Fort Fisher 1865

The Photographs of T.H. O'Sullivan

Chris E. Fonvielle Jr.

Chris E. Fonvielle Jr.

To Frank Ward III, who shares my interest in the Civil War.

Burlington, NC
November 16, 2019

SlapDash Publishing, LLC
Hampstead, North Carolina

MW01257616

FORT FISHER 1865

THE PHOTOGRAPHS OF T.H. O'SULLIVAN

Chris E. Fonvielle Jr.

625 Hickory Point Road, Hampstead, NC 28443 • 910.232.0604 • slapdashpublishing@me.com • www.carolinabeach.net

LIBRARY OF CONGRESS CONTROL NUMBER: 2010936896
Chris E. Fonvielle Jr.
Fort Fisher 1865 - The Photographs of T.H. O'Sullivan
Hampstead, N.C., SlapDash Publishing, LLC.
128 pp.

ISBN: 978-0-9792431-8-9

Second Printing: December 2016

Designed and produced by Daniel Ray Norris (SlapDash Publishing, LLC). Software: Adobe InDesign, Photoshop, Illustrator and other Adobe products. Apple Macintosh computers and Canon imaging products were used in the proofing and production of this book.

Table of Contents

Dedication

To Thomas Meares Green (left), my best friend for as long as I can remember. Here we are in 1968.

Foreword

By 1865, Timothy H. O'Sullivan was one of the most rugged, field-worn photographers of the Civil War. And he was only twenty-five years old.

O'Sullivan started in photography as a teenager, working for Mathew Brady, one of the most famous photographers in the booming field. It was Brady's mission to document the great war in photos. To that end, he sent O'Sullivan with the U.S. Navy on one of the war's first amphibious operations in the South in the autumn of 1861. O'Sullivan took some of the first images of occupied territory after Beaufort, South Carolina, was captured in November 1861.

The following year O'Sullivan was at Cedar Mountain, Virginia to photograph the freshly scarred battlefield there. In 1863, now working for Alexander Gardner, O'Sullivan was at Gettysburg, Pennsylvania, photographing the dead of both sides. When General U.S. Grant took his army across the Rapidan River in early May 1864 to begin his relentless march on Richmond, Virginia, O'Sullivan was there, too.

For four long years, O'Sullivan took his "what is it?" darkroom wagon to the battlefields and forts, and into Union army camps. He shared the same rugged conditions as soldiers, slogging through the mud during bone-chilling winters and swatting the infernal flies in the heat of summer. Through it all he exposed hundreds of plates, and in the process took some of the most famous photographs of the Civil War.

And yet, in the waning months of the war, when offered the opportunity to go on one more adventure—to photograph the recently captured Fort Fisher on the North Carolina coast—O'Sullivan did not hesitate. Thus North Carolina's most famous Civil War battlefield came to be thoroughly documented in a series of about forty images by one of America's most prolific photographers.

As was typical of Civil War photographers, O'Sullivan left us little in the way of documentary evidence about his life. His Civil War journeys are known principally through his images. Reportedly, he was at Hampton Roads, Virginia in December 1864 to photograph the U.S. Navy fleet preparing to sail toward Fort Fisher, but there is no evidence that O'Sullivan ventured to southeastern North Carolina until he photographed the earthen stronghold in early February 1865.

Using both a "large plate" camera for 7 x 9-inch glass plates and the twin-lens stereoscopic camera to produce 4 x 10-inch stereo glass plates, O'Sullivan methodically documented Fort Fisher in photographs. He never bothered to make a detailed list of exactly what images he took. The negatives and their paper sleeves, often inscribed with handwritten titles and captions, were the only key to O'Sullivan's work. His Fort Fisher negatives remained a part of Alexander Gardner's vast collection of Civil War images until the Library of Congress acquired them in 1944.

Although fairly complete, the thirty-one extant T.H. O'Sullivan negatives of Fort Fisher—eighteen large plates and thirteen stereoscopic (half stereo) plates at the Library of Congress—represent only a portion of his photographic work at Fort Fisher. While taking advantage of the high quality scans available of the extant negatives of the Fort Fisher photographs, Fonvielle has tapped other sources: original stereo view cards, and in the case of one photo, digging up the only known reproduction from an undated early twentieth century newspaper.

This book, *Fort Fisher 1865: The Photographs of T.H. O'Sullivan*, presents for the first time all of the thirty-nine known O'Sullivan photos of Fort Fisher and the immediate vicinity, and two of the U.S. Navy's task force assembled to attack the fort. After more than three decades of studying Fort Fisher's history, Dr. Chris E. Fonvielle Jr. has reassembled the most complete photographic record of O'Sullivan's images of Fort Fisher known to exist. Barring new discoveries (which is always a possibility), O'Sullivan's photographic record of Fort Fisher is presented here in its entirety.

Bob Zeller
www.civilwarphotography.org

Acknowledgments

From 1979 to 1983, I served as the last curator of the Blockade Runners of the Confederacy Museum at Carolina Beach, North Carolina. The privately owned and operated museum, which opened in 1967, was the dream of the late John H. Foard. A native of Wilmington, North Carolina, Mr. Foard had always been fascinated with the role his hometown played as the Confederacy's most important seaport during the Civil War. In 1982, five years after Mr. Foard's death, his beloved Blockade Runner Museum collection was purchased by New Hanover County, and moved to the Cape Fear Museum in Wilmington early the following year.

One of the more exciting displays at the former Blockade Runner Museum was a large interactive diorama depicting Fort Fisher, the Confederacy's strongest seacoast fortification and the main guardian of Wilmington. A state-of-the-art sound and light show took visitors through the fort's history, from construction to capture. Flanking the diorama on both sides were copies of thirty-six photographs of Fort Fisher taken by Timothy H. O'Sullivan shortly after the fort's fall to Union forces in January 1865. As an enthusiast of Civil War photography, I was familiar with O'Sullivan views of Fort Fisher published in Alexander Gardner's *Photographic Sketchbook of the War* (Washington, D.C., 1866), Francis T. Miller's ten volume *Photographic History of the Civil War* (New York, 1911), and on display at the Fort Fisher State Historic Site. Born and raised in Wilmington, I spent many hours exploring the remains of Fort Fisher. Until I went to work at the Blockade Runner Museum, however, I had no idea that T.H. O'Sullivan had taken so many photographs of the imposing fortress.

I became entranced by O'Sullivan's images, and studied them closely to learn more about Fort Fisher's construction, armament, defenders, and captors. My keen interest soon led me on a quest to discover if there were additional O'Sullivan views of Fisher not on display at the Blockade Runner Museum. Indeed there were, although not as many as I had hoped. After thirty years of searching, I uncovered only another five scarce photographs in the Library of Congress, the New York Historical Society, and in an early twentieth century Wilmington newspaper. *Fort Fisher 1865: The Photographs of T.H. O'Sullivan* comprises the most complete assemblage of the only extant wartime images of the mighty earthen stronghold to date.

I deeply appreciate the assistance and support for this project from the following friends and institutions: Jonathan Anderson; Barbara Baker; Ray Flowers, Becky Sawyer, and Jim Steele of the Fort Fisher State Historic Site; Adaire Graham; Josh Howard; the late Albert Jewell; Chadwick Johnson; Jim Keith; Paul Laird; James B. Legg; Library of Congress; Jim McKee of the Brunswick Town/Fort Anderson State Historic Site; Torrey McLean; New York Historical Society; Alan Purdie; Joseph Sheppard of the New Hanover County Public Library; Tonia Smith; Dan Sturdevant; Jay Taylor; Beverly Tetterton; Frank Vattelana; and the late Marvin Willett. Special thanks goes to Daniel Ray Norris, master book designer and president of SlapDash Publishing and NC Starburst Press; Bob Zeller, co-founder and president of the Center for Civil War Photography, who kindly wrote the Foreword to *Fort Fisher 1865: The Photographs of T.H. O'Sullivan*; and my wife Nancy.

Chris E. Fonvielle Jr.
Wilmington, North Carolina

Photo by Daniel Ray Norris

The Fort

Union soldiers occupying Fort Fisher most likely paid little attention at first to the two civilians wandering around the fortification. They kept to their assigned tasks—repairing the fort's damaged earthen walls and timbered palisade and remounting cannon atop the high sandy ramparts. Curiosity eventually got the best of them, however, as they periodically halted their work to observe the men moving about with a small wagon, occasionally stopping to set up a curious-looking wooden box on a tripod to "make a likeness," as the saying went in those days, of the fort's imposing features.

The civilians were, in fact, the "photographic artist" Timothy H. O'Sullivan and his unidentified assistant, employees of Alexander Gardner, himself a renowned Civil War era image-maker. Gardner had been contracted by the U.S. Army to make a photographic record of Fort Fisher that had only recently been captured by a Union combined operation. Gardner dispatched O'Sullivan to Fort Fisher on the Cape Fear River in southeastern North Carolina to do the field work. There, in early February 1865, O'Sullivan took at least thirty-nine images of Fort Fisher and its immediate vicinity, making it at the time one of the most photographed Confederate forts. Some Union occupation troops, probably at O'Sullivan's request, posed for his camera, and thus became part of Fort Fisher's fascinating photographic history themselves.

Fort Fisher was the largest and strongest seacoast fortification in the Confederacy, and the main guardian of Wilmington, North Carolina, the South's most important seaport for most of the Civil War. Union and Confederate observers alike deemed Fort Fisher virtually impregnable. Unlike conventional fortifications, Fisher's massive ramparts were made of beach sand. Up to that time America's coastal fortifications had been built mostly of brick and stone to protect its seaports against foreign invasions. Fort Caswell on Oak Island that guarded Wilmington from the mouth of the Cape Fear River, and Fort Macon near Beaufort, North Carolina were typical of the antebellum masonry forts built along both the Atlantic and Gulf coasts. By the 1860s, however, such forts had been made obsolete by improved weaponry. Heavy artillery bombardments could pound such defenses into rubble, as was the case when Union forces attacked Fort Pulaski near Savannah, Georgia in April 1862. From that point on, Confederate forts were constructed mostly of dirt and sand, which could be displaced but not destroyed by artillery fire.

Confederate engineers designed networks of earthen defenses to protect Wilmington and other key cities from capture. By the summer of 1863, when Union forces put Charleston, South Carolina under siege warfare, Wilmington's importance grew. Merchants transferred much of their operations from Charleston, where maritime trade was now uncertain, to Wilmington 175 miles up the coast. Various types of sailing ships and steamships imported essential supplies from Europe into the Confederacy by way of Wilmington to meet the needs of soldiers on the battlefront, as well as civilians on the home front. To get supplies in, however, these vessels had to run a gauntlet of Union ships blockading the Cape Fear River.

Lacking the industrial facilities necessary to produce sufficient quantities of military arms and equipment, the Confederacy looked to Europe, especially Great Britain, to help meet its wartime needs. President Abraham Lincoln hoped to prevent a seaborne trade from developing between the Confederacy and European nations when he proclaimed a naval blockade of the Southern states shortly after the war began in April 1861.[1]

Gleason's Pictorial Drawing-Room Companion, July 16, 1853

Wilmington was North Carolina's largest city and busiest port in 1860. By the summer of 1863, it was the most important seaport in the Confederacy.

Declaring a blockade and enforcing it, however, were two different matters. The U.S. Navy was initially plagued by too few ships, logistical problems of supply and fueling, a lack of strong political support, and Europe's ambiguity about the legality of the blockade. Moreover, the 3,549-mile-long coastline from Virginia to Texas, and the dozen major seaports and smaller harbors and inlets that blockade-runners could access, made it all but impossible to halt Confederate waterborne commercial activity.

Southern buyers and European suppliers established shipping firms to handle the overseas smuggling trade that ensued. In exchange for Southern commodities—mostly cotton—the Confederacy imported firearms, artillery, ammunition, swords, bayonets, wool cloth for uniforms, blankets, shoes, medicines and food for the armies, as well as civilian goods.

By 1865, more than 1,600 ships of all classes—schooners, sloops, and steamships foremost among them—had been employed as blockade-runners. Approximately 1,300 of them were sailing vessels, used until 1863-1864, when the blockade had tightened to the extent that it became difficult to break it by wind power alone. Side-wheel and screw propeller steamers were used more often in the last two years of the war, relying upon speed and stealth to challenge Union blockaders hovering around the entryways to Southern harbors and cruising the shipping lanes. At least 106 different blockade running steamers with names like *Banshee, Bendigo, Hebe, Night Hawk, Phantom, Ranger,* and *Wild Dayrell* enjoyed a phenomenal success rate of about 80 percent at Wilmington, despite the increasingly heavy blockade.

Blockade running proved to be a lucrative trade as shipping companies and investors made substantial profits selling or auctioning blockade-run goods. Profits often came at a high price, however. Many merchant vessels were captured or destroyed by blockaders as they attempted to enter or exit Southern seaports, and lives sometimes lost. The famous Confederate spy Rose O'Neale Greenhow drowned off the blockade-runner *Condor* trying to run the blockade of Wilmington in the early morning hours of October 1, 1864.

Union blockading ships off Fort Fisher

Harper's Pictorial History of the Civil War, September 24, 1894

By war's end, more than 1,450 blockade-runners had been captured or destroyed by the U.S. Navy. About sixty blockade-runners were wrecked along the Cape Fear coast, and the skeletal remains of some of them can still be seen just offshore at low tide, including the *General Beauregard* and the *Ranger*. More times than not, however, blockade-runners eluded their pursers to make their port-of-call.[2]

The blockade-runner *Alice*   Courtesy of Charles V. Peery estate

The steamer *Alice* was one of the most successful blockade-runners that traded at Wilmington. Built as the *Sirius* by Caird and Company of Greenock, Scotland in 1857, she measured 231 feet in length, 26 feet in width, and drew about 13 feet of water. The Importing and Exporting Company of South Carolina purchased the *Sirius* in 1863, and converted her into the blockade-runner *Alice*. She ran the blockade twenty-four times, including nine documented trips into Wilmington, without getting caught.[3]

Wilmington offered great advantages for blockade-runners like the *Alice*. The Tar Heel port was located near the neutral British transshipment points of Bermuda and Nassau in the Bahamas. Vast quantities of supplies were transported on large ocean-going merchant ships from England to Bermuda and Nassau, where they were transferred to smaller vessels for the final dash into the Confederacy. Blockade-runners could enter the Cape Fear harbor by one of two passageways—Old Inlet at the mouth of the river, and New Inlet, a shallow passageway six miles to the northeast. The dual entryways were separated by Bald Head Island and Frying Pan Shoals, making the distance between the inlets about forty miles on the outside of the estuary.

Wilmington itself was twenty-eight nautical miles from the mouth of the Cape Fear River, and thus far out of range from Union naval artillery. Moreover, the seaport had good lines of communication throughout the southeast. The river was navigable to Fayetteville, eighty-two miles upstream from Wilmington, and three railroads tapped the seaport. The most important of these rail lines was the Wilmington and Weldon Railroad, a major supply route for General Robert E. Lee's Army of Northern Virginia. More ships ran the blockade at Wilmington than all other Southern seaports combined. Little wonder that by 1864 Southerners considered Wilmington *the lifeline of the Confederacy*.[4]

Wilmington's growing significance led the Confederate government to rigorously defend it. Next to Charleston, Wilmington became the most heavily fortified place along the

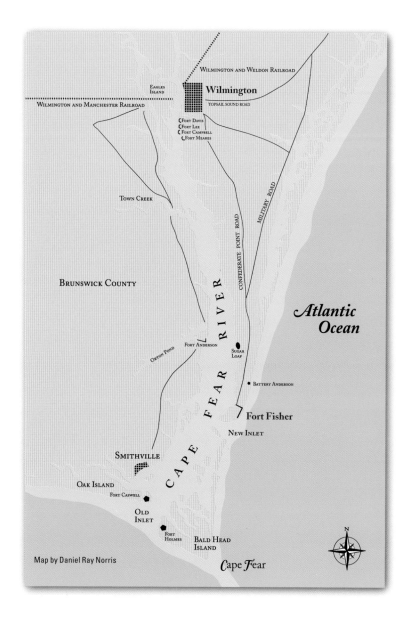

Map by Daniel Ray Norris

Anderson, built atop the ruins of the colonial port of Brunswick on the west side of the Cape Fear River. The largest and best-armed forts, however, were built to safeguard the river entrances used by blockade-runners. Forts Caswell and Campbell and Battery Shaw on Oak Island, and Fort Holmes on Bald Head Island overlooked Old Inlet, while New Inlet was guarded by Fort Fisher. New Inlet was created by a severe storm in early September 1761, that cut through a narrow stretch of beach called the "Haulover" near the tip of New Hanover County. One hundred years later, New Inlet became the most popular passageway for blockade running ships at Wilmington.

The tapered peninsula above New Inlet was called Federal Point, flanked by the Atlantic Ocean on the east side and the Cape Fear River to the west. Southerners renamed it Confederate Point during the war. There, twenty miles south of Wilmington, engineers began constructing defenses in the spring of 1861. On April 28, Major Charles Pattison Bolles began building two artillery batteries about one mile north of the New Inlet. Bolles, who had recently been appointed chief engineer of the Cape Fear

Library of Congress

Battery Bolles, the first artillery position built on Confederate Point in the spring of 1861.

Atlantic coast. Strong earthen defenses virtually surrounded the city, while auxiliary works stretched up and down the river and along the beaches. The strongest interior work was Fort

Author's collection

**Captain William Lord DeRosset,
Wilmington Light Infantry**

River and its approaches, erected a large sand battery close to the seashore, with a direct line of fire on the inlet, and a smaller work further up the beach.[5]

About one week after arriving on Confederate Point, Bolles was transferred across the harbor to oversee the construction of an artillery battery on Oak Island at Old Inlet. He was replaced as commander on Confederate Point by William Lord DeRosset, a member of one of the Cape Fear's oldest and most prominent families and captain of the Wilmington Light

Infantry. The militia unit was the first company of troops to garrison Confederate Point, where it arrived on May 7, 1861. DeRosset remained in charge there only ten days or so, but long enough to strengthen Bolles' largest battery by arming it with two 24-pounder smoothbore cannons and adding fifty yards of breastworks on each side. In recognition of the work's architect, Captain DeRosset christened it Battery Bolles.[6]

Construction of defenses on Confederate Point progressed in fits and starts throughout 1861-1862, as engineers came and went. At least six different gray-uniformed officers designed or supervised the military project in the first sixteen months of the war as authorities transferred them, as they had Major Bolles, to other places. The same was true of Major William Henry Chase Whiting, one of the Confederacy's top engineers who served as inspector general of North Carolina's coast defenses as of April 23, 1861, headquartered in Wilmington, but was sent to Virginia only three weeks later. Work also slowed during the war's first summer as the military established Camp Wyatt, a large Confederate camp of instruction 1.5 miles north of Battery Bolles.

On August 31, 1861, state authorities placed Sewell Fremont, superintendent of the Wilmington and Weldon Railroad and colonel of the 1st Corps of North Carolina Volunteer Artillery and Engineers, in charge of the state's coastal defenses from New River in Onslow County southward to the South Carolina line. Like Whiting before him, Fremont focused on building batteries to guard the Cape Fear River inlets and Wilmington.[7]

Courtesy of Robert J. Cooke

Colonel Sewell Fremont

Wilmington Daily Journal, September 14, 1861

April 12-14, 1861, but promptly resigned his commission after that first battle of the war to join the Confederate Engineer Corps. Meade succeeded Captain Winder as engineer on Confederate Point.[8]

On September 13, 1861, Sewell Fremont named the defenses Fort Fisher, in honor of Colonel Charles F. Fisher, commander of the 6th Regiment North Carolina State Troops who was killed "while gallantly leading his men" at the battle of First Manassas, Virginia, on July 21, 1861.[9]

North Carolina Troops, 1861-'65

Colonel Charles F. Fisher, 6th N.C. State Troops, Fort Fisher's namesake

The overall plan for defenses on Confederate Point, as initially laid out by Major Whiting, was a cordon of gun batteries from Battery Bolles up the beach to a line of tall sand dunes, which would eventually be reconfigured to form a great work across the peninsula from the ocean to the river. Under Fremont's supervision, Captain John C. Winder of the North Carolina Engineers, erected additional works on Confederate Point, including a large casemate battery—an underground chamber with embrasures for cannons—about 350 yards north of Battery Bolles. The casemate battery was later named Battery Meade. Its namesake, Lieutenant Richard Kidder Meade Jr., had fought for the U.S. Army at Fort Sumter in Charleston harbor,

Colonel Fremont resigned from active military duty in January of 1862 to resume full-time work with the Wilmington and Weldon Railroad. His replacement at Fort Fisher was Captain John J. Hedrick, a dry goods salesman from Wilmington who had led the Cape Fear Minute Men in the untimely seizures of two U.S. Army forts—Johnston and Caswell—at the mouth of the Cape Fear River in early January 1861, more than four months before North Carolina seceded from the Union. It was the first overt act against the federal government in North Carolina during the crisis of the Union. Hedrick took over command at Fort Fisher in January 1862, and served until late June of that year. He continued the military construction projects on Confederate Point, now under the overall direction of Brigadier General Samuel Gibbs French, commander of the District of the Cape Fear from mid-March until mid-July 1862.[10]

Colonel William Lamb of the 36th Regiment North Carolina Troops (2nd N.C. Artillery), assumed command of Fort Fisher on July 4, 1862. After touring what he defined as works that "amounted to nothing," he determined to strengthen and expand the defenses so that they could withstand the heaviest bombardment of the U.S. Navy. A lawyer and newspaper editor from Norfolk, Virginia, Lamb had little experience building forts before he arrived on Confederate Point. Lamb had formerly commanded Fort St. Philip (renamed Fort Anderson in 1863) at Brunswick Point across the Cape Fear River. There he became interested in military engineering. When W.H.C. Whiting returned to Wilmington in November 1862 as a general officer and new commander of the District of the Cape Fear, he supported

Courtesy of Larry Croom

Colonel William Lamb,
Confederate commander of Fort Fisher, 1862-1865

Colonel Lamb's ambitious plans for reconstructing Fort Fisher. Under Whiting's close supervision, Lamb transformed Fisher from a scattering of sand batteries into the mightiest seacoast fortress in America. He worked his laborers six days a week, and seven days a week when rumors of attack reached him. Construction of the defenses took place under the watchful eye of Union blockaders off New Inlet that occasionally lobbed shells onshore in an effort to disrupt the work parties. Undeterred, Lamb pressed on.

By 1864, Fort Fisher was a massive two-sided sand fortification that looked like a giant number "7" from a birds-eye view. A series of elevated gun batteries mounting forty-five cannons was connected by a broad sand rampart and stretched for more than a mile. Thousands of cubic feet of sand were piled up one shovel full, one wheelbarrow load at a time by Confederate soldiers working alongside African American laborers.

The fort's land front—the short shank of the "7"—guarded the northern land approaches. Beginning near the Cape Fear River at Shepherd's Battery, the defensive line stretched eastward for approximately 698 yards, according to Colonel Lamb's calculations, toward the Atlantic Ocean where it formed a full bastion. The sandy rampart, sodded with luxuriant marsh grass to prevent erosion, was twenty-four feet high from ground level to the top, or parapet, of the fort at an angle of 45 degrees, and about 127 feet thick at the base. The parapet was interspersed with sixteen gun chambers mounting en barbette (elevated so as to fire over the top of the fort) twenty-one guns—a 24-pounder; 6.4-inch, 32-pounder Navy guns; 8-inch and 10-inch Columbiads; and a 24-pounder Coehorn mortar. Two additional mortars were placed on the parade ground below. Each gun chamber was separated by a traverse, a large mound of sand approximately ten feet higher than the parapet, designed to protect cannons and crews from enfilade fire and flying shrapnel. Underneath the fort's embankment was a series of interconnected bunkers, each serving alternately as an ordnance and gunpowder magazine or a bombproof, where soldiers could seek refuge during a bombardment.

A nine foot high palisade of heavy sharpened pine timbers pierced with loopholes for musketry, and a minefield supplemented the land face defenses. Engineers also cut a tunnel, technically called a postern, underneath the rampart halfway down the line so that light artillery and sharpshooters could be deployed into a demilune constructed just outside, but connected to, the fort's main wall. This position would allow the fort's defenders to fire into the flanks of attacking enemy troops. To provide a field of fire for the gunners, the woods were cleared for half-a-mile north of the land face. The road to Wilmington ran along the riverbank as it approached the fort at Shepherd's Battery.

The land and sea face batteries intersected at a full bastion about 100 yards from the ocean's high water mark. Located in the northeast corner of the fort, this immense thirty-two-foot high battery was appropriately called the Northeast Bastion. An 8-inch Columbiad and a British manufactured 8-inch Blakely rifle comprised the battery's armament. From the Northeast Bastion the defensive line ran southward, paralleling the oceanfront for 1,898 yards.

A seventy-five-yard four-gun emplacement, built in the same massive style as the land face batteries, connected to the Northeast Bastion. Joining this was the casemated Battery Meade, but

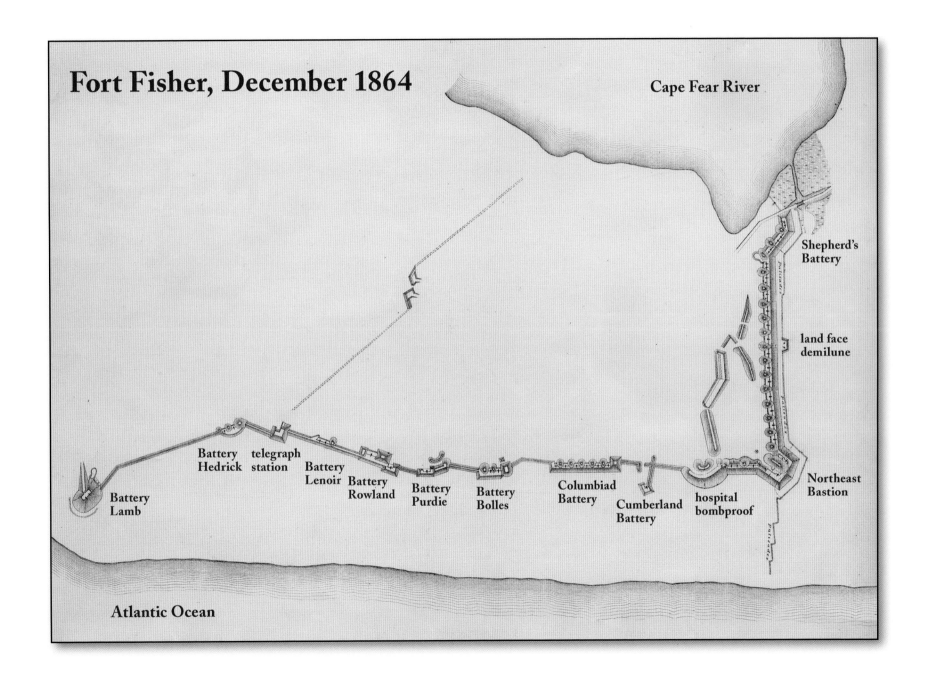

Fort Fisher, December 1864

Cape Fear River

Shepherd's Battery

land face demilune

Northeast Bastion

hospital bombproof

Cumberland Battery

Columbiad Battery

Battery Bolles

Battery Purdie

Battery Rowland

Battery Lenoir

telegraph station

Battery Hedrick

Battery Lamb

Atlantic Ocean

converted by Colonel Lamb into a bombproof hospital. From there a series of nine batteries mounting eighteen seacoast guns were connected by an immense curtain of sand. These batteries were also flanked by traverses, but stood lower than the land face batteries, as they were designed for ricochet firing at enemy ships.

At the far south end of the sea face towered a forty-three foot high conical gun emplacement named Battery Lamb for the fort's commander, but generally referred to as Mound Battery. Its massive profile could be seen for miles at sea, and blockade-runners depended on it for both navigation and protection from its two large cannons as they approached New Inlet.

From Battery Lamb to the south tip of Confederate Point was an open expanse of low, sandy ground. At the extreme point, engineers constructed a large, elliptical four-gun battery that commanded New Inlet. Built in the autumn of 1864, Battery Buchanan was named in honor of Admiral Franklin Buchanan of the C.S. Navy who had recently been captured at the naval battle of Mobile Bay, Alabama. The battery was also a citadel to which Fort Fisher's garrison might retreat if necessary, and from where survivors could be transported to safety across the Cape Fear River or reinforcements landed. A wharf to accommodate even large steamships was located near Battery Buchanan.[11]

Blockade running sailors often referred to Colonel Lamb and his Tar Heel artillerists as their guardian angels. Many times during the war their booming cannons turned away pursuing enemy gunboats, allowing blockade-runners safe passage into the harbor by way of New Inlet.

Both Colonel Lamb and General Whiting believed that a mighty fortress like Fort Fisher was needed to defend Wilmington against a Union land and sea attack they were certain would eventually come to the shores of the Cape Fear coast. Whiting most feared a land assault on the north side of Wilmington, where the defenses were weakest, or by a Union amphibious landing at Wrightsville Beach or Topsail Sound and an advance against the city from the east, thus bypassing the big forts at the mouth of the river. By the autumn of 1864, however, the enemy's attack plans became known. Fort Fisher was their target. Lamb hoped he had prepared well for battle, as much was at stake.

"Fort Fisher, commanding the New Inlet entrance to Cape Fear River, the British steamer *Hansa* running the blockade under the guns of the fort."

Illustrated London News, January 23, 1864

The Battles

For most of the war, President Abraham Lincoln's administration and the U.S. War Department paid less attention to the coastal war than to the ground war, determined as they were to capture the Confederate capital of Richmond and other strategic cities. Of the South's seaports, only Charleston, South Carolina, where the war began, and New Orleans, Louisiana, the South's largest city and busiest seaport, had attracted much popular and political interest in the North. Union forces captured New Orleans in late April 1862, and placed Charleston under siege the following spring. In the meantime, Union sailors on board blockading ships off Wilmington watched in frustration as Confederate commerce vessels smuggling vital supplies came and went almost at will. Despite its best efforts, the U.S. Navy seemed powerless to halt the illicit trade at the Tar Heel seaport. The navy desperately needed the assistance of a U.S. Army expeditionary force to help close Wilmington to blockade running.

Not until the mid-summer of 1864 was U.S. Secretary of the Navy Gideon Welles able to convince President Lincoln to support a combined operation against Wilmington. The navy had proposed several plans for attacking Wilmington earlier in the war, but none of them had generated the necessary political backing. Then, on August 5, 1864, Union naval forces sealed Mobile Bay, Alabama, the last open port on the Gulf of Mexico. That left Wilmington as the only major Confederate seaport still accessible to trade with the outside world. While Lincoln gave Welles' proposal the green light, he deferred final approval of it to the U.S. Army's commanding officer, General Ulysses S. Grant.

Grant initially expressed little enthusiasm for committing a large expeditionary force to assist the navy in attacking Wilmington. As far as he was concerned, his soldiers should remain in Virginia to keep the pressure on General Robert E. Lee. Since the late spring of 1864, Grant's operational forces—the Army of the Potomac and the Army of the James—had been slugging it out with Lee's Army of Northern Virginia around Petersburg and Richmond. Despite the heavy fighting, neither side had been able to break the deadlock. Grant saw no reason to detach upwards to 10,000 troops for an amphibious assault 240 miles away in southeastern North Carolina when they were more needed in his ranks. Gideon Welles argued that the stalemate in Virginia could be broken by denying Lee's army the military arms, equipment, and food coming into the Confederacy by way of Wilmington. "Could we seize the forts at the entrance of Cape Fear and close the illicit traffic, it would be almost as important as the capture of Richmond on the fate of the Rebels, and an important step in that direction," the navy secretary declared. As political pressure grew, Grant finally consented to detach an expeditionary force to assist the navy in closing the Carolina seaport, although he set no timetable. He promised only to release them "when the time was right."[1]

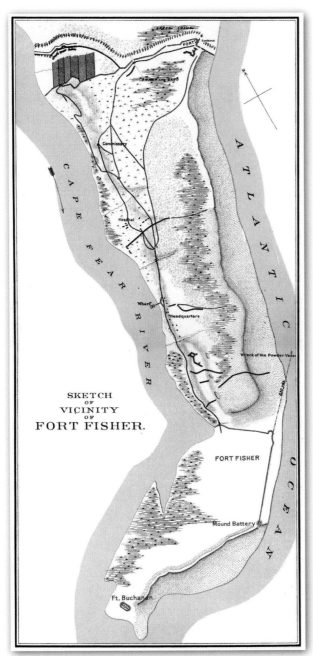

SKETCH
OF
VICINITY
OF
FORT FISHER.

The Official Military Atlas of the Civil War

To maintain the pressure, Rear Admiral David D. Porter, the newly assigned commander of the North Atlantic Blockading Squadron, assembled the largest naval task force of the war for operations against Fort Fisher. Sixty-four warships, including the navy's largest frigates—*Colorado, Minnesota, Powhatan, Susquehanna,* and *Wabash*—as well as an array of steam sloops and screw steamers gathered at Hampton Roads, Virginia. The fifty-five-gun *Colorado* alone mounted more ordnance than all of Fort Fisher's emplaced cannons. Complementing these well-armed ships were four monitors—essentially floating tanks with revolving iron-plated turrets—and the most powerful ship in the U.S. Navy, the *New Ironsides*, a massive, tortoise shaped vessel covered with thick iron plating.

Admiral Porter figured it was going to take all the heavy firepower he could muster to demolish his target—Fort Fisher, the strongest seacoast fortification in the Confederacy. Although the Navy Department had considered an alternative plan for attacking the forts at Old Inlet and then moving up the Cape Fear River to strike Fort Fisher from the rear, Porter argued that capturing Fort Fisher at New Inlet would deny blockade-runners access to the harbor through either passageway. Vessels that entered through Old Inlet to the south could not get upriver to Wilmington's docks once Fort Fisher was in Federal hands.[2]

While the U.S. Navy assembled its forces for the fall campaign and waited on Grant to provide troops for the expeditionary force, blockade-runners continued to trade at Wilmington. Even so, captures of the merchant vessels occurred more frequently, as the U.S. Navy now had only the Tar Heel seaport with which to concern itself.

With Wilmington now the South's only open port, the Confederate commerce raiders *Tallahassee* and *Chickamauga* also began using the harbor as a base of operations. This gravely concerned General Whiting who believed that the appearance of commerce raiders, in addition to the attention blockade-runners already attracted, would provoke an all-out Union attack on the seaport. But Whiting's protests fell on deaf ears with Confederate President Jefferson Davis, who argued that the *Tallahassee* and the *Chickamauga* had nowhere else to go but Wilmington for refitting and coaling. More than ever, Whiting became convinced that an assault on the city was inevitable and he warned Colonel William Lamb at Fort Fisher to make ready.[3]

Sure enough, in October 1864, sound intelligence reached Confederate military authorities that Federal forces were indeed planning to strike Wilmington. Rather than leave the seaport's protection in the hands of General Whiting, the man most responsible for planning and supervising the construction of the city's formidable defenses, however, President Davis replaced him with General Braxton Bragg, the most vilified officer in the Confederate army. Few Southerners placed much faith in Braxton Bragg, who had a reputation for being difficult and incompetent. One person who did, and the only one who mattered in the end, was Jefferson Davis. When the *Richmond Enquirer* learned of the change in command, it announced: "General Bragg is going to Wilmington. Goodbye Wilmington." Whiting and his men were devastated and morale dropped among Wilmington's defenders at a very critical hour, just as Bragg arrived in the city in late October.[4]

The politics of command also haunted Federal forces. General Grant had hand-picked Major General Godfrey Weitzel to lead a 6,500-man expeditionary force comprised of Brigadier General Adelbert Ames' Second Division, 24th Army Corps, and two brigades of U.S. Colored Troops, commanded by Brigadier General Charles J. Paine of the Third Division, 25th Army Corps, Army of the James, for the Fort Fisher expedition. But Weitzel's superior officer, Major General Benjamin F. Butler, commander of the Union Department of Southeastern Virginia and North Carolina, finagled his way into taking over effective command. Grant was inexplicably intimidated by Butler and did not intervene on Weitzel's behalf, much to Admiral Porter's chagrin. There was bad blood between Porter and Butler that went back to the early years of the war. Success in the impending attack on Fort Fisher depended on perfect harmony between the U.S. Navy and U.S. Army, yet the two service branch commanders intensely disliked each other. It did not bode well for the mission.

Admiral Porter was eager to proceed toward the target, but was delayed by the army. General Butler had proposed a novel feature for the attack—a giant floating bomb. His idea was to pack a ship with 300 tons of gunpowder, run it ashore at Fort Fisher and detonate it. Butler believed that the simultaneous explosion of such an immense quantity of gunpowder would create tornado force winds capable of blowing down the sand walls of the mighty fortress, stun its defenders, and allow the Union army to march in and sweep up the survivors. As farfetched as it seemed to some ordnance experts, to others it was a plan worth trying, especially if it saved the lives of good Union men. The USS *Louisiana*, a steamship patrolling Pamlico Sound, North Carolina, was chosen for the suicide mission. Butler spent much of the autumn of 1864 preparing his pet project for demolition.

Admiral Porter's grand armada and General Butler's army transports finally sailed from Hampton Roads on December 13, with plans to meet off the Cape Fear coast a few days later. But the navy's arrival at the rendezvous point was impeded by a stopover at Beaufort, North Carolina, to take on more supplies and ammunition, and by bad weather. Butler's ships tried to ride out the gale off Fort Fisher as they waited for the navy, but soon had to put into Beaufort themselves to replenish their stocks of coal and water and allow soldiers to recover from seasickness.

As the army transports refitted, Porter proceeded toward Fort Fisher. When Butler did not reappear within a short time, Porter carried out the attack plan without him. Hoping to steal his rival's thunder, Porter deployed the powder vessel *Louisiana* without Butler on the scene. It was a win-win situation for the contentious admiral. If it succeeded, the navy was on hand to reap the laurels of success. If it failed, Porter could blame Butler for wasting valuable time, money, and resources on the ill-fated project.

Harper's Weekly, January 28, 1865

General Benjamin F. Butler's powder ship *Louisiana*

As it turned out, the *Louisiana,* loaded with only 215 tons of gunpowder, did nothing more than make enough noise to awaken Fort Fisher's slumbering garrison when it blew up after midnight on Christmas Eve. "There's a fizzle!" remarked Commander Alexander C. Rhind of the USS *Agawam.* "The powder boat proved an ignominious failure," added Lieutenant Commander Thomas O. Selfridge Jr. of the USS *Huron.* Admiral Porter then determined to reduce Fort Fisher the old-fashioned way—naval bombardment.[5]

The sight was both spectacular and unnerving to Confederate soldiers manning their artillery batteries onshore. Sixty-four Union warships slowly advanced toward Fort Fisher on a dark gray Christmas Eve morning in 1864, each one ready for battle. "A grander sight than the approach of the armada towards the fort was never witnessed on our coast," recalled Colonel William Lamb.[6]

The survival of both Wilmington and the Confederacy depended upon the survival of Fort Fisher. General Robert E. Lee had recently sent word to Confederate commanders in Wilmington that if the city fell, "he could not maintain his army." Since the late spring of 1864, Lee's Army of Northern Virginia had been engaged in a war of stalemate and attrition against Union forces led by General U.S. Grant for possession of Petersburg, Virginia. Like two stubborn fighting dogs, the armies were locked in savage combat with neither side showing any signs of giving up. But with far fewer soldiers and supplies, the prolonged fighting was taking a heavier toll on Lee's beleaguered army. Much of the military supplies and provisions keeping Lee's men alive and in the trenches came from Wilmington, thus accounting for the commanding general's dire message that the seaport must remain in friendly hands or his army and the Confederacy were doomed. Colonel Lamb understood the desperate challenge he faced at Fort Fisher.[7]

The *New Ironsides* "opened the ball" at 12:40 p.m. Christmas Eve by firing a big 11-inch shell at the imposing sand fort. Colonel Lamb answered with a 10-inch Columbiad from one of his sea face batteries. This rather harmless exchange opened the most intensive artillery battle of the Civil War. No one who participated in or observed the first battle of Fort Fisher had ever seen anything like it. In fact, warfare had never seen anything like it. Commander Daniel Ammen of the USS *Mohican* spoke for most participants, both Union and Confederate, when he wrote: "It has not been my lot to witness any operation comparable in force or in effect to the bombardment of Fort Fisher." For two days, December 24-25, Union warships pounded the massive earthen fort with 20,271 shot and shell. The air was filled with shrieking projectiles of all types and sizes (from 3-inch bolts to 15-inch cannonballs that weighed more than 300 pounds), clouds

Battles and Leaders of the Civil War

Fort Fisher's Mound Battery returns fire on the Union fleet.

of white smoke and geysers of sand from exploding shells, and the pungent odor of sulphur. The deafening peal of heavy ordnance reverberated across the sea with such stunning effect "that the ocean fairly trembled," remarked one Federal soldier. The roar was "like the rattling of a thousand railway trains," echoed a comrade. It was the largest naval bombardment in American history up to that time and its outcome would determine how much longer the Civil War lasted.[8]

Bursting shells soon set wooden barracks and buildings on fire and demolished Colonel Lamb's brick headquarters inside Fort Fisher, but otherwise caused surprisingly little damage to the earthworks and few casualties among the garrison. As Lamb and Whiting intended, both the stout defenses and defenders held their own. Assisting Lamb inside the fort was General Whiting, who had come voluntarily to the fort to act as an advisor to his protégé and serve as a combatant. His presence inspired the gray-uniformed soldiers who greatly admired and respected the man they called "Little Billy" because of his diminutive stature.

During the height of the first day's bombardment, Colonel Lamb noticed that the enemy's gunboats seemed to be concentrating their fire on the fort's flags, the most visible targets from seaward. The main flagstaff got so chewed-up that the garrison standard could not be raised. Lamb sent word to Captain Daniel Munn at Mound Battery on the south end of the sea face to hoist a flag there. The battery's flagpole was not equipped with halyards, prompting Private Christopher C. "Kit" Bland of Company K,

36th Regiment North Carolina Troops, to volunteer to shinny up the staff to attach the flag. The courageous soldier quickly drew the wrath of Union warships, as they threw numerous iron shells in his direction. Miraculously, Bland escaped unhurt and even repeated his daring deed amid the cheers of both his comrades and enemy sailors on board the ships when the end of the flag was cut loose by incoming projectiles. The flag flew over Mound Battery throughout the remainder of the battle and was afterward presented to North Carolina's governor, Zebulon B. Vance.[9]

After the failure of his powder boat experiment, General Butler was in no mood to cooperate with Admiral Porter who, he believed, had deliberately sabotaged the project to make him look foolish. Consequently, after returning from Beaufort, Butler put ashore only one-third of his 6,500-man infantry force above Fort Fisher on Christmas Day. A reconnaissance unit, led personally by General Weitzel, advanced down the beach but soon reported that, despite the intensity of the navy's bombardment, neither Fort Fisher nor its armament had been damaged enough to warrant a ground assault. An attack against the still strong defenses, Godfrey Weitzel concluded, would be suicidal. Still seething with anger at Porter, Butler pondered Weitzel's report and decided to abort the mission altogether. He withdrew his troops from onshore and sailed back to Virginia.[10]

Colonel Lamb and General Whiting were stunned to see the Union army retreat just as it seemingly prepared to attack Fort Fisher. They were also pleasantly surprised at the withdrawal of the enemy's fleet on December 27. The Confederates realized that the battle was over, for the time being at least, and that they had won. Great celebration ensued inside the fort and at Wilmington.

General Bragg, who claimed much of the credit for the victory at Fort Fisher, although he had remained in Wilmington during the battle, received a new gray uniform from his admirers in the city. On January 12, 1865, he staged a grand review for civilian dignitaries of Confederate reinforcements—a division of more than 6,400 troops led by Major General Robert F. Hoke—that Robert E. Lee had sent from Virginia to help defend Wilmington. But Bragg's overconfidence concerned Whiting and Lamb, both of whom were convinced that the Federals were not yet done with Fort Fisher. They fully expected a renewal of the Union attack at an early date.[11]

In the North, the failed expedition sparked a firestorm of controversy that led to a Congressional investigation as to the causes, as well as the dismissal of Benjamin Butler from the army. Disappointed by Butler's performance, General Grant relieved him from command and sent him home to Massachusetts. Then Grant got serious about renewing the attack on Fort Fisher.

Indifferent though he may have been toward the first expedition, Grant now took a keen interest in taking Wilmington. The December defeat at Fort Fisher had been offset by a concurrent victory on the Georgia coast. After capturing Atlanta in early September 1864, Major General William T. Sherman led his 60,000-man army virtually unopposed across the state later that autumn, capturing Savannah in late December. He presented the city to President Lincoln as a Christmas gift.

Glad to see Sherman safe on the seacoast, Grant was now eager to transfer his troops by ships to Virginia to reinforce his own armies on the Petersburg-Richmond front. But Sherman had another plan in mind. He proposed to march his legion to Virginia by way of the Carolinas, destroying supply depots and railroads along the way. If need be, he could strike Wilmington from behind. At any rate, Sherman believed that his advance would ultimately force Robert E. Lee to abandon his entrenched position at Petersburg and into open ground where Grant and Sherman could converge on and demolish his army.

Sherman's plan and his confidence in it greatly encouraged Grant. The crowning achievement might well be the defeat of the Confederacy and the end of the four-years-long war. He authorized Sherman to begin his "Northern expedition" (historians call it the Carolinas Campaign) as soon as possible.

Having agreed to Sherman's bold plan, Grant determined to guarantee its success by furnishing his trusted ally with reinforcements and supplies, or a haven on the seacoast halfway between Petersburg and Savannah where he could retreat in case he got into trouble. Wilmington now took on a whole new meaning for Grant. Possession of the Cape Fear River and the

An 1865 Currier and Ives lithograph, "The Victorious Attack on Fort Fisher, NC, Jan. 15th, 1865, by the Fleet Under Rear Admiral D.D. Porter and Troops Under Genl. A.H. Terry."

city's railroads would enable him to forward men and supplies to Sherman once he reached North Carolina. Wilmington must be captured![12]

As Sherman prepared for his grand march into the Carolinas, Grant renewed the attack on Wilmington, with Fort Fisher as the first target. Once the stronghold had been taken, Union forces would advance up the Cape Fear River against Wilmington, the real objective this time around. Grant replaced the deposed Butler with the affable Brigadier General Alfred H. Terry, commander of the 24th Army Corps, Army of the James, to lead the expeditionary force. Terry's Provisional Corps, as it was officially designated, comprised the troops from Butler's failed attack plus Terry's old brigade from the First Division, 24th Army Corps, and support personnel for a total of about 9,600 men.

Porter's warships and Terry's transports reached Fort Fisher late on the night of January 12, 1865. Earlier that day Braxton Bragg had put his troops on parade near Wilmington and thus was unprepared to contest the landing of Federal troops on Confederate Point the following morning. By the time Bragg and his musket-bearers reached the peninsula on January 13, the enemy was already onshore and making preparations to assault Fort Fisher.

British war correspondent Frank Vizetelly's original composite sketch of the devastating effects of the Union naval bombardment on Fort Fisher's Northeast Bastion, January 1865.

Some Union warships provided covering fire for General Terry's troops, while others kept up a fierce bombardment of Fort Fisher. For two-and-a-half days, January 13-15, 1865, the fleet fired 19,682 projectiles in what turned out to be the second largest naval bombardment of the Civil War. Porter instructed his gunners to knock-out the fort's land face cannons that protected the ground across which the army planned to advance. The admiral also determined that his naval forces should participate in the ground assault. On the morning of January 15, he sent ashore 2,261 volunteer sailors and Marines from the slightly scaled-down fleet of fifty-eight ships..

Colonel Lamb and General Whiting kept their men at the cannons as best they could, but the intense enemy shelling soon drove them into the fort's bombproofs. At one point during the battle on January 15, Lamb counted 100 navy shells exploding in his fort in one minute's time. Nothing and no one could withstand that kind of barrage from bursting iron projectiles. More than 300 of Lamb's men were killed and wounded, and an increasing number of cannons dismounted or disabled.

General Whiting repeatedly sent dire messages about the deteriorating situation inside the fort to General Bragg, who was now with Hoke's division dug in along a strong line of trenches near Sugar Loaf hill, four-and-a-half miles north of Fort Fisher. Whiting implored Bragg to send reinforcements to the fort and to attack the Union troops south of Sugar Loaf. Inexplicably, Bragg did not attempt to reinforce the fort's beleaguered garrison until after sunrise on January 15, and then by landing troops of General Johnson Hagood's South Carolina brigade at Battery Buchanan near New Inlet. With Hagood's steam transport in plain view of the Union fleet, gunboats immediately redirected some of their fire toward it and drove off the Confederate vessel after fewer than 500 soldiers had landed. No more was heard from Bragg during the battle.

After almost three days of heavy naval bombardment, the Union ground assault was ready to begin late on the afternoon of January 15. By then the U.S. Navy had done sufficient damage to Fort Fisher's defenses, dismounting or destroying all but one cannon on the land front—an 8-inch Columbiad in the Northeast Bastion—that covered the beach, and blowing holes in the palisade. Porter's warships simultaneously blew their steam whistles to signal the advance at 3:25 p.m. About 3,200 blue-uniformed soldiers of General Adelbert Ames' division rushed toward the fort's battered western rampart, while Porter's naval column pushed down the sea beach. The sailors and Marines were met by blistering musketry from 500 Confederate soldiers personally commanded by both Colonel Lamb and General Whiting mounted atop the Northeast Bastion. In less than thirty minutes, the Confederates had killed or wounded almost 300 seamen, and forced the survivors to retreat back up the beach.

Although Porter's men failed to breach the defenses, their efforts distracted the attention of a large portion of the fort's garrison and enabled the Union army to establish a foothold on the land

Brigadier General Alfred H. Terry, U.S. Army

Le Monde Illustré, 1865

"Assault of 15 January 1865 on Fort Fisher by infantry troops of the Federal army."

front's weakly defended west end. Bragg's reinforcements from Hagood's Brigade that had entered the fort early that morning failed to respond to Colonel Lamb's order to support the 250 North Carolina soldiers at Shepherd's Battery. The Tar Heels were outnumbered by more than ten-to-one when Union forces stormed the rampart. General Whiting led a fierce counterattack in an attempt to drive the Federal troops off the fort, but he was severely wounded in the action and removed from the battlefield.

About half-an-hour after Whiting went down, Colonel Lamb rallied his men for another counterattack but he was also badly wounded. He did not return to the battle either. Battle for possession of Fort Fisher now became a soldiers' fight. Hand-to-hand combat and firefights of musketry raged for hours on both the land face mounds and the parade ground below.

By about 9:00 p.m., the remnants of the vastly outnumbered, outgunned, and out-of-luck garrison evacuated the fort and retreated toward Battery Buchanan at the tip of Confederate Point. There they hoped to be evacuated by boats to the safety of the west side of the Cape Fear River. But Confederate sailors and Marines stationed at Buchanan had prematurely abandoned the battery, taking all of the boats with them. [13]

The garrison, including the wounded Lamb and Whiting, had little choice but to await their fate. Pursuing Union troops caught-up with them about 10:00 p.m. that night, January 15, 1865. General Alfred Terry personally accepted the surrender of General Whiting, who was lying on a stretcher in the sand. Taken prisoner along with about 2,000 of his comrades, Whiting died of complications of his wounds two months later in a military prison in New York. On his deathbed, he wrote a scathing report of Braxton Bragg's inaction in the defense of Fort Fisher and the last Confederate seaport of Wilmington. Colonel Lamb survived his wound and returned to Wilmington from time to time in the postwar years, where he was considered the "hero of Fort Fisher."

The Federal victory at Fort Fisher ended Confederate blockade running, and the capture of Wilmington five weeks later helped assure the success of General William T. Sherman's Carolinas Campaign. The fall of the South's strongest fort and its principal seaport was of immense significance. "We had some very important naval victories during the war, but none so important as Fort Fisher," boasted Admiral Porter. "Its fall sealed the fate of the Confederacy."[14] No longer were supplies able to reach the Army of Northern Virginia. As he had predicted if Wilmington fell, Robert E. Lee could no longer "maintain his army." He evacuated his position at Petersburg in early April, and retreated westward. General U.S. Grant followed close behind, catching the Confederates at Appomattox Courthouse, Virginia. There Lee surrendered the remnants of his once proud army on April 9, 1865. Two weeks later, Confederate forces in North Carolina, commanded by General Joseph E. Johnston, including Bragg's forces that had abandoned Wilmington, surrendered to General Sherman at Durham Station, effectively ending the long and bloody war.

The Photographer

Union forces that captured Fort Fisher and war correspondents were mightily impressed with the size and strength of the massive earthen stronghold. "I have since visited Fort Fisher and the adjoining works, and find their strength beyond what I have conceived," Admiral David D. Porter wrote in his official report of the battle. "The work. . .is really stronger than the Malakoff Tower, which defied so long the combined power of France and England [in the Crimean War]." E.S. of the *New York Tribune* wrote that: "No description can convey an adequate idea of the stupendous strength and almost Titanic proportions of the combined works of Fort Fisher, Mound Fort, and Fort Buchanan."[1]

While surveying the recently captured works, Brevet Brigadier General Cyrus B. Comstock, chief U.S. Army engineer at Fort Fisher, wrote to John A. Rawlins, General U.S. Grant's chief of staff, "wishing" that a photographer be sent "down here to take a few photographs of Fort Fisher. It is the only way to give a good idea of it." Rawlins passed along Comstock's request to Grant, who in turn sent a memo on January 24, 1865, to Major General George G. Meade, commander of the Army of the Potomac, asking him to direct "Col. Duane to send his Photographers to Fort Fisher to report to Gen. Comstock for duty until the works about Cape Fear are photographed."[2]

The photographer working for Colonel James C. Duane, chief engineer of the Army of the Potomac, was Alexander Gardner, one of the most renowned image-makers of the Civil War. No additional army correspondence or government contract for the Fort Fisher photographic project has been discovered, although it is known that Gardner dispatched one of his best photographers, Timothy H. O'Sullivan, to make a photographic record of the imposing defenses.

Historians know little about O'Sullivan's life beyond his work as one of America's early premier photographers. He was of Irish descent. His parents—Jeremiah and Ann O'Sullivan—left Ireland to escape the

Library of Congress

T.H. O'Sullivan, photographer of Fort Fisher in 1865.

potato famine in the 1840s. His father claimed that his son was born in Ireland about 1840, but Timothy later claimed to have been born on Staten Island, New York. Wherever his place of birth, by the time O'Sullivan was a teenager, he was apprenticing in the New York portrait gallery of Mathew Brady, the country's most famous photographer. He soon transferred, however, to Washington, D.C., to work in Brady's satellite studio managed by Alexander Gardner.

When the Civil War broke out, Brady sent young O'Sullivan out to the battlefields, where he captured some of the conflict's most poignant images. He was with the Union army at Beaufort and Port Royal, South Carolina in 1861, and in northern Virginia the following year. In 1863, now in the employ of Alexander Gardner, O'Sullivan took some of his most famous wartime photographs in the aftermath of the battle of Gettysburg, Pennsylvania. O'Sullivan was with the Army of the Potomac in the siege fighting around Petersburg, Virginia in 1864, and from there traveled to southeastern North Carolina to photograph Fort Fisher.[3]

A news dispatch by Thomas M. Cook, a *New York Herald* war correspondent imbedded with the U.S. Army in the Lower Cape Fear, placed O'Sullivan at Fort Fisher in early February 1865, less than three weeks after the stronghold's capture. "Messrs. Gardner & Company, the army photographers, have been sent here by General Grant to make a series of views of Fort Fisher and other works in this vicinity for the embellishment of the Lieutenant General's report," Cook reported. "The series will embrace thirty or forty pictures [and] will be the most interesting series the war has produced." Cook mistakenly identified the photographer "now here taking the negatives" as "W.H. Sullivan." Photographic evidence suggests that T.H. O'Sullivan completed his work at Fort Fisher in two or three days.[4]

WILMINGTON.

Mr. Thomas M. Cook's Despatch.

FORT FISHER, Feb. 4, 1865.

PHOTOGRAPHS OF THE CAPTURED REBEL WORKS.

Apropos of General Terry's report, I had nearly forgotten to mention that Messrs. Gardner & Company, the army photographers, have been sent here by General Grant to make a series of views of Fort Fisher and the other works in this vicinity for the embellishment of the Lieutenant General's report. Mr. W. H. Sullivan, for a long time with the headquarters of the Army of the Potomac, is now here taking the negatives The series will embrace thirty or forty pictures. If permission shall be granted to multiply pictures from these negatives, Messrs. Gardner & Co., will find it a difficult task to satisfy the public demand for them. They will be the most interesting series the war has produced.

New York Herald, February 8, 1865

This *New York Herald* news dispatch misidentified T.H. O'Sullivan as W.H. Sullivan.

After the war, O'Sullivan took some of the most enduring photographs of the American West. He was the official photographer with the U.S. Geological Exploration of the Fortieth Parallel, 1867-1869, led by Clarence King, and then accompanied Lieutenant George M. Wheeler's survey of the One Hundredth Meridian, 1871-1874. O'Sullivan died of tuberculosis, probably at age forty-one, on Staten Island, New York, on January 14, 1882, only one day shy of the seventeenth anniversary of the fall of Fort Fisher.

Nomenclature

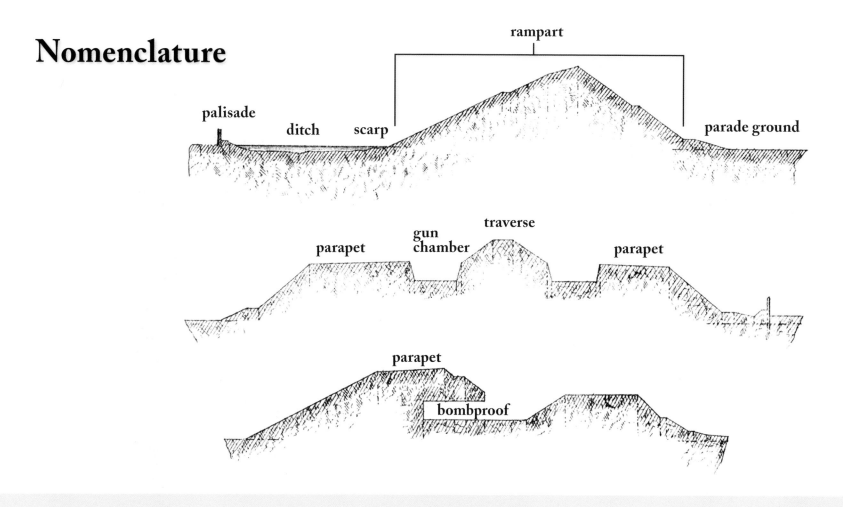

palisade   ditch   scarp   rampart   parade ground

parapet   gun chamber   traverse   parapet

parapet   bombproof

Timothy H. O'Sullivan's composite view of Fort Fisher's land face batteries in 1865

24-pounder cannon mounted *en barbette*

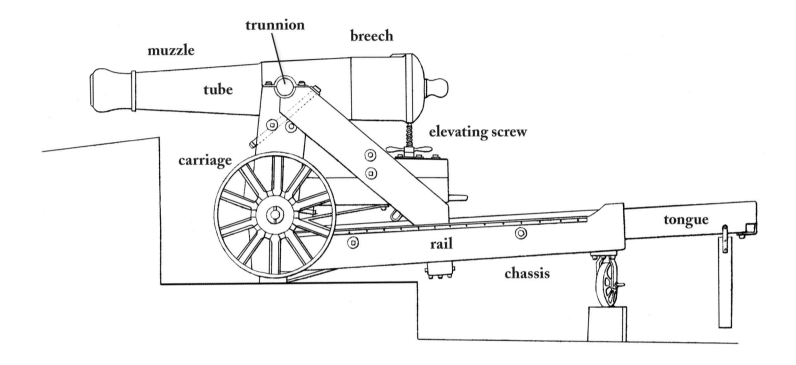

trunnion

breech

muzzle

tube

elevating screw

carriage

tongue

rail

chassis

Fort Fisher U.S. Naval Task Force in Hampton Roads, Virginia

According to records in the Prints and Photographs Collections in the Library of Congress, the repository for T.H. O'Sullivan's original glass plate negatives of Fort Fisher, this photograph (LC-B817-7432)* shows Rear Admiral David D. Porter's naval task force set to embark from Hampton Roads, Virginia, on its Fort Fisher expedition in mid-December 1864. Sixty-four warships comprised the largest fleet assembled during the Civil War. At least seventeen side-wheelers and steam sloops appear in the image, as well as the USS *New Ironsides* (on the horizon slightly right of center). Predecessor to the modern day battleship, the *New Ironsides* was a massive tortoise shaped vessel with 3-inch to 4.5-inch thick iron plating covering her sides. She was difficult to maneuver and unseaworthy, but considered invincible to enemy fire. Her armament consisted of twenty large cannons, fourteen of which were 11-inch Dahlgren smoothbores. Even so, the *New Ironsides'* ordnance comprised only a fraction of the 627 total cannons in the armada of warships.[1]

* Photograph numbers herein prefixed with LC are in the holdings of the Library of Congress, Washington, D.C.

USS *New Ironsides*

Author's collection

Fort Fisher U.S. Naval Task Force in Hampton Roads, Virginia (b)

Eight steamships are seen in this O'Sullivan image (LC-USZ62-79429) titled "Fort Fisher Expedition in Hampton Roads, Virginia." The vessels appear to be underway, and the fuzzy image of a launch can be seen near the beach on which O'Sullivan stood when he took the photograph. A spit of sand outlines the horizon.

A host of war correspondents and sketch artists representing some of the country's leading newspapers accompanied Admiral David D. Porter's fleet in December 1864. There is no evidence that O'Sullivan went along, although this and the previous photograph suggests that he was present at Hampton Roads, headquarters of the North Atlantic Blockading Squadron, at about the time the grand armada sailed toward the Cape Fear. Even if he did, O'Sullivan never went ashore as Federal forces failed to capture Fort Fisher in the first attack.

Is it possible that these photographs of Porter's warships were made after their return to Virginia from the victorious Union expedition to Fort Fisher in January 1865? Indeed, O'Sullivan did not travel to Fort Fisher until early February 1865, more than two weeks after the fort fell. Perhaps he photographed vessels that had participated in the recent attack, and just prior to his departure for the Cape Fear.

Com. D. D. Porter U.S.N.
Hero of Fort Fisher,

Author's collection

Batteries (gun emplacements) 1-5, including Shepherd's Battery

From right to left, looking southward in this image, are gun batteries 1-5, separated by traverses, on the west end of Fort Fisher's land face. Batteries 1-3 comprised a half bastion known as Shepherd's Battery. A lone Union soldier stands atop the fort's parapet at battery 2, and cannon muzzles are visible in batteries 3, 4, and 5.

About 3,200 Federal troops in three brigades of Brigadier General Adelbert Ames' Second Division, 24th Army Corps, rushed across the open sandy ground as they attacked this section of the fort late on the afternoon of January 15, 1865. By then the defenses had been greatly weakened by the U.S. Navy's intense two-and-a-half day bombardment, which disabled or destroyed the heavy artillery covering the land approaches to the fort, and blew gaps in the palisade.

Many Union soldiers were killed in the advance or shortly after surmounting the fort's rampart, and wooden headboards on the sandy ridge on the far right of the photograph mark the final resting place of some of them. A man in civilian clothes, perhaps T.H. O'Sullivan himself, stands near the palisade in the center background.

Graves of Union soldiers outside Shepherd's Battery

Land Face Batteries
(Exterior)

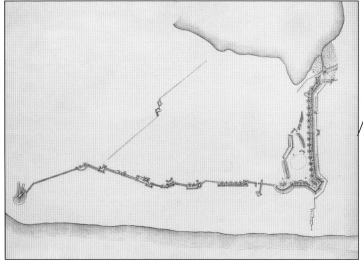

Batteries 1-4

Photo by Daniel Ray Norris, January 1, 2011

Land Face Batteries
(Exterior)

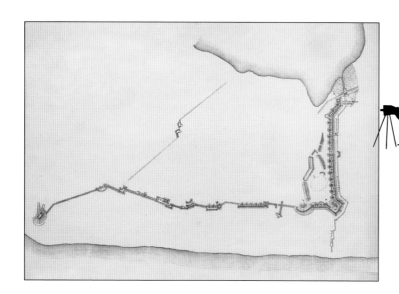

An alternate view of Fort's Fisher western-most land defenses. O'Sullivan's original glass plate negative apparently has been lost, but this grainy photograph—extracted from an undated early twentieth century Wilmington, North Carolina newspaper—reveals a distinctive image (showing batteries 1-4, from right to left). It was taken slightly closer to the fort than the image on page 36, and shows five Union soldiers standing atop battery 2.

Shepherd's Battery

Exterior view of Shepherd's Battery (batteries 1-3) looking southward toward Fort Fisher's west flank, adjacent to the Cape Fear River. The battery's namesake has been lost to history. Perhaps because of its isolated position when it was first built in late 1861 or early 1862, the garrison thought the battery resembled a shepherd's retreat. Colonel William Lamb enlarged and strengthened it after assuming command of Fort Fisher on July 4, 1862.[2]

The effects of the heavy Union naval bombardment—craters on the fort's rampart and beach, and the severely damaged timbered palisade—are clearly visible in this photograph (LC-B817-7572). Note the civilian, perhaps O'Sullivan, standing halfway up the rampart between the first and second traverses.

Damaged palisade and cannons in battery 3

Land Face Batteries
(Exterior)

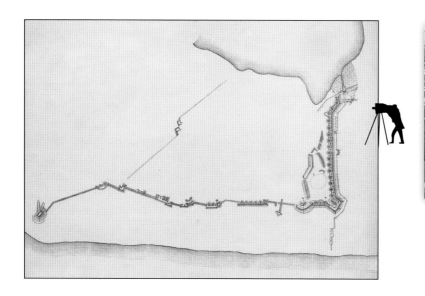

Photo by Daniel Ray Norris, January 1, 2011

Batteries 1-5(b)

O'Sullivan took this photograph (LC-B817-7480) slightly closer to batteries 1-5 than the image on page 36, but at a later time. The image clearly shows the palisade now repaired from the destructive naval bombardment. Union occupation forces, supervised by the 15th New York Engineers, spent several weeks restoring Fort Fisher to guard against a potential Confederate counterattack. Even as O'Sullivan took his photographs, military operations were still ongoing in the Lower Cape Fear. Three Confederate brigades of Major General Robert F. Hoke's division were strongly entrenched along the Sugar Loaf lines four-and-a-half-miles north of Fort Fisher, facing the recently promoted Brevet Major General Alfred H. Terry's Provisional Corps encamped two miles above the fort.

Repaired palisade and cannons in battery 3

Land Face Batteries
(Exterior)

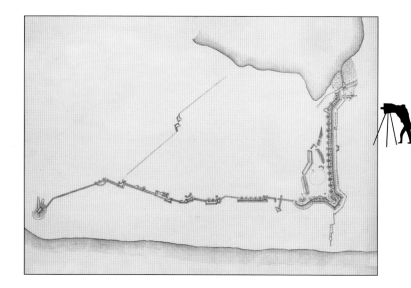

Batteries 5-10, Demilune and Postern

Moving eastward along Fort Fisher's land face, this photograph (LC-B817-7168) shows batteries 5-10 (from right to left). Cannon muzzles peek over the parapet in batteries 7-10. Note the heavy damage to the rampart and traverses from the Union naval bombardments.

The image also shows a demilune (to the left) in front of the fort's postern. A demilune (sometimes termed a ravelin) formed a salient angle on the outside of the main fortification so as to cover the scarp and rampart. Two 12-pounder Napoleon cannons and riflemen were deployed in Fort Fisher's demilune, located halfway between Shepherd's Battery and the Northeast Bastion, to provide enfilade fire on Union ground forces on January 15, 1865.

Confederate troops came and went by way of the postern, a tunnel cut through the land face, marked in the photograph by the wooden lintel below the traverse on the far left.

The silhouettes of three Union soldiers are barely discernible to the left of the cannon in battery 7. They were standing there as O'Sullivan began exposing his glass plate negative, but moved away before their full likenesses could be captured in the time lapse photograph, leaving behind only ghostly shadows. There are, however, three additional soldiers in the image. Two of them sit on the parapet at the bottom of the second traverse on the right, while another sits almost directly underneath them, on the outside of the fort along the palisade.

On the sandy plain in front of the demilune are eight wooden headboards marking the graves of some of the fallen from the battle. The Fort Fisher State Historic Site's Visitor Center occupies this area today.

Land Face Batteries
(Exterior)

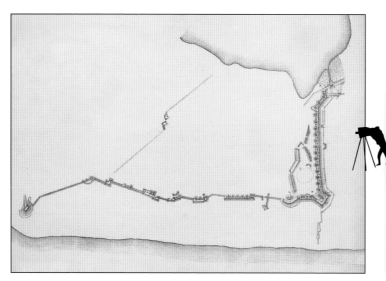

Batteries 6-10 and Demilune

O'Sullivan moved his camera closer to the fort to capture batteries 6-10 and the demilune in this view (the only known positive image of which is in the holdings of the New York Historical Society, New York). Cannon muzzles can be seen in batteries 7-9. Craters and holes on both the rampart and traverses are also evident. Large iron fragments of exploded navy projectiles litter the beach in the foreground, which is also pockmarked with footprints. Five Union soldiers stand atop the demilune to the left, and two of them ham it up for O'Sullivan's camera by pretending to be boxing. The head and chest of a sixth soldier can be seen to their right.

Union soldiers atop Fort Fisher's land face demilune

Land Face Batteries
(Exterior)

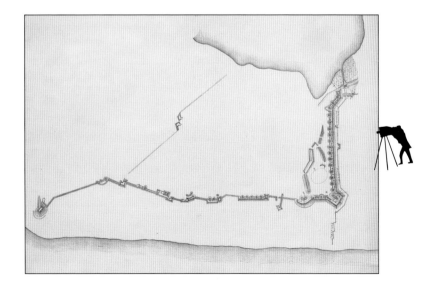

Batteries 10-13

Moving further down Fort Fisher's land front, O'Sullivan photographed batteries 10-13 (from right to left) in this view (LC-B817-7170). Cannons can be seen protruding from gun emplacements 10, 12 and 13. The cannon in battery 12 in the center of the picture was a banded 6.4-inch rifle. Battery 13 to the left, bolstered by a strong wooden revetment on the twelfth traverse, is armed with a Confederate 7-inch Brooke rifle. Colonel Lamb mounted it on January 12, 1865, the same day, as it turned out, that the Federal fleet returned to renew its attack on Fort Fisher. Two shovels stick out of the parapet to the left of the Brooke rifle.[3]

Three large cannonballs dot the ground in front of the land face. The nine-foot-tall pine palisade appears to decline in height on the left, but it is just an illusion. O'Sullivan propped his camera on a sandy ridge that dropped off at a dug out area just in front of batteries 13-15. Soldiers had created a deep ditch in excavating sand for the fort's massive rampart.

Four Union soldiers appear in the image: three on top of the fort and another in a prone position, resting on his right side, in front of the palisade below the second traverse on the right.

Photo by Daniel Ray Norris, January 1, 2011

Land Face Batteries
(Exterior)

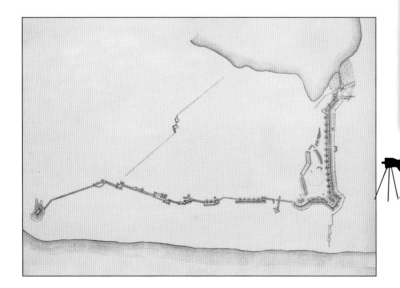

Batteries 14-16 and the Northeast Bastion

A morning sun blinds the details of Fort Fisher's land defenses near the Atlantic Ocean. From right to left are batteries 14-16 and the Northeast Bastion, where the fort's land and sea faces intersected. Deep craters and displaced sand from the Federal navy's bombardments mar the landscape along the rampart. Wagon ruts cut the beach in the foreground, and two 15-inch cannonballs and iron fragments dot the sand ridge.

A group of soldiers (left of center) are gathered on the fort's parapet near the Northeast Bastion. On the Northeast Bastion (far left) is a mounted 8-inch Columbiad, with four or five soldiers standing near its muzzle. Unlike all the other cannons in the land face batteries, which were disabled or dismounted by the focused fire of the Union warships during the January 1865 battle, the Northeast Bastion's 8-inch smoothbore gun remained active.

8-inch Confederate Columbiad in the Northeast Bastion

Land Face Batteries
(Exterior)

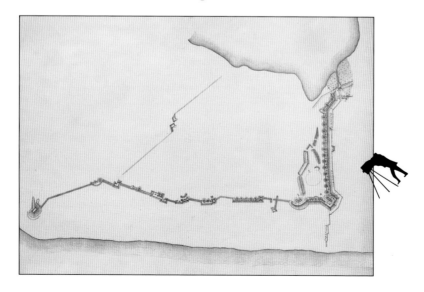

Northeast Bastion

Fort Fisher's land and sea face defenses joined at this imposing thirty-two foot high work in the northeastern corner of the fort. Appropriately called the Northeast Bastion, its armament consisted of an 8-inch Columbiad and a British-manufactured 8-inch Blakely rifle that had been imported through the Union blockade. Batteries 15 and 16 are to the right, with the muzzle of a 10-inch Columbiad pointing skyward in battery 16.

Admiral Porter dispatched a landing party of 2,261 sailors and Marines—volunteers from various warships in the fleet—to attack the Northeast Bastion in cooperation with the U.S. Army's advance against the western land defenses. The naval assault turned disastrous. In less than thirty minutes after it began at 3:25 p.m. on January 15, 1865, almost 300 blue-uniformed seamen lay dead and

Battles and Leaders of the Civil War

Assault of the Union naval column on Fort Fisher's Northeast Bastion.

wounded on the beach seen here, casualties of heavy rifle-musketry from 500 Confederates commanded by both Colonel William Lamb and Major General W.H.C. Whiting. They mounted the fort's parapet to fire down into the blue-uniformed sailors and Marines as they approached the Northeast Bastion. Seamen who survived the onslaught turned their backs on the fort and bolted back up the beach.[4]

The bodies of the fallen and most of the battle debris had been picked-up by the time O'Sullivan took this photograph in early February 1865, although a half-buried 15-inch cannonball and fragments still litter the beachfront. O'Sullivan's "what is it?" darkroom wagon stands in the center background, just in front of the repaired timbered fence. Four Union soldiers sit atop the Northeast Bastion to the far left.

Land Face Batteries
(Exterior)

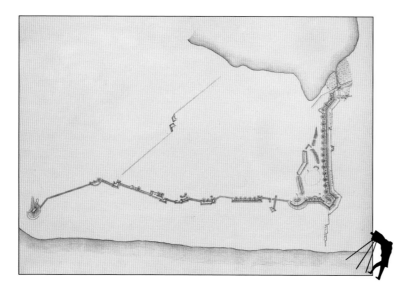

Shepherd's Battery

O'Sullivan made several interior views of Shepherd's Battery, a half bastion adjacent to the Cape Fear River, where some of the heaviest fighting occurred as the Union army breached the defenses on January 15, 1865. This photograph, which O'Sullivan took while standing in the mucky marsh along the river shore, shows the devastating effects of the Union navy's bombardments on the battery's gun emplacements 1-3 (left to right).

A disabled U.S. Navy 6.4-inch, 32-pounder sits askance on its carriage on the terreplein of battery 1 to the left, and the carriage of another cannon rests on the ground below. A U.S. Navy 8-inch shell gun is lodged against the wooden revetment of battery 2, while a sister gun and carriage lie against the battery's interior slope at the bottom of the stairway. Partially obscured from view by the second traverse is an 8-inch Columbiad in battery 3. A 30-pounder Parrott rifle points over the parapet of battery 3.

Three bombproof doors can be seen: one underneath the first traverse, and two in the large embankment (formerly a gunpowder magazine) underneath the traverse of battery 3. What appears to be two crates for rifle-muskets lie on either side of the bombproof door of battery 3 on the far right.

Several soldiers are visible in this view. One man, right hand on his hip, stands atop the parapet of battery 1. A second soldier sits on the terreplein just to the left of the stairway and Parrott rifle in battery 3. A third man looks toward the camera as he stands on the ledge between the bombproof entranceways of battery 3. The heads and shoulders of at least two other soldiers can barely be made out in a ground pit between the stairways leading up to batteries 2 and 3.

An enormous partially hewed pine log rests near the foreground, with a large discarded wheel from a sling cart used for moving heavy cannons behind it.

Land Face Batteries
(Interior)

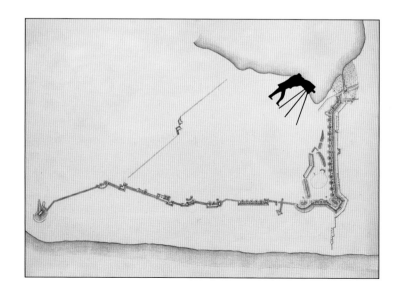

Shepherd's Battery (b)

Photo by Daniel Ray Norris, January 1, 2011

Land Face Batteries
(Interior)

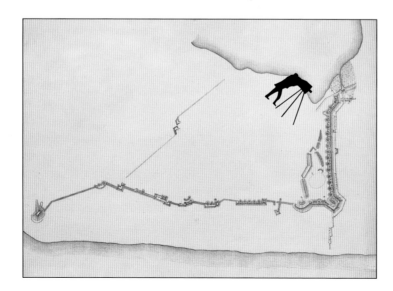

O'Sullivan probably took this photograph (LC-IDG-12599) soon after the previous one. It is basically the same view of the interior of Shepherd's Battery as seen on page 54, but with a few subtle differences. With a slight adjustment to his camera lens, O'Sullivan captured a little less of the palisade on the left, and the foreground appears to be drier. The soldiers in the previous photograph have either departed or changed positions. Two soldiers to the left of the flagpole curiously observe O'Sullivan at work, while three others, two of whom have their backs to the camera, chat at the palisade.

Shepherd's Battery (c)

Land Face Batteries
(Interior)

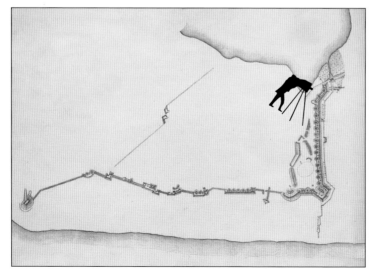

This stereoscopic view (LC-B815-1229) also shows the backside of Shepherd's Battery, although it was taken sometime after the previous two images. Note that the spokes of the sling cart wheel and lower steps leading up to gun emplacement 2 have now been removed, probably by soldiers for use as firewood. It was, after all, early February. A lone sentinel stands just to the right of the stairway of battery 2, looking toward the camera.

Battery 1

This may be T.H. O'Sullivan's most famous photograph of Fort Fisher (LC-B817-7196). It is a close-up view of gun emplacement 1 in Shepherd's Battery, revealing substantial damage to the ordnance. Although still atop its carriage on the battery's terreplein, a disabled rifled and banded U.S. Navy 6.4-inch, 32-pounder gun has been turned on its side. A 10-inch Columbiad, one of its trunnions knocked-off, lies in the pool of water at the bottom of the battery. It had occupied the open space to the left of the 32-pounder on the terreplein until dismounted during the December 1864 battle.

An 8-inch Columbiad to the right of the 10-inch Columbiad was apparently being readied for mounting in the gun chamber. Laborers using ropes would have pulled the artillery piece up to the terreplein on the boards laid

Land Face Batteries
(Interior)

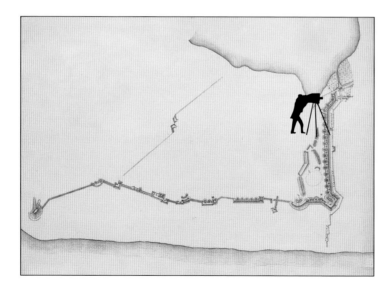

against the battery's interior slope to the left of the stairway. Two gun chassis lie upside down near the Columbiads, while a gun carriage sits upright in front of the opening in the palisade on the far left.

The opening in the palisade became known as the "Bloody Gate," as heavy combat occurred there on January 15, 1865. Lacking a timbered gate, it was defended by a bronze 12-pounder Napoleon smoothbore cannon that fired canister into the right flank of Union army forces advancing on the fort along the Wilmington Road. A bridge crossed a low muddy area just outside Shepherd's Battery, but the Confederates had removed its planks to prevent the enemy from entering the fort in that direction. Forced to shift eastward to escape the deadly fire of the Napoleon, Union troops gained a foothold on the fort by storming up Shepherd's Battery and overwhelming the vastly outnumbered Tar Heel defenders in the gun chambers. The Federals then swarmed onto the parade ground below to capture the Napoleon field piece from behind. This allowed successive blue-clad units to enter Fort Fisher through the Bloody Gate.[5]

In addition to the four Federals on the parapet, a heavyset soldier, his rifle-musket slung over his right shoulder, stands guard at the bombproof door.

O'Sullivan displayed his flair for photographic artistry by capturing the reflection of a soldier and the 32-pounder gun on the terreplein in the pool of water.

Battery 2

O'Sullivan took two photographs of the second gun chamber of Shepherd's Battery, looking eastward along the land face toward the Atlantic Ocean in the far left background. The first image seen here (LC-B8171-7195), shows a dismounted U.S. Navy 8-inch chambered shell gun, one of its trunnions broken off, lying against the wooden revetment underneath the shadowed traverse. The wheeled carriage cheeks were also dislodged from the chassis.

Stands of iron canister (sometimes referred to as grapeshot) with wooden cup sabots still attached and ammunition boxes are still stacked against the front revetment underneath the line of sand bags. The partially buried barrel nearby contained water for dipping a sheepskin-covered ramrod, which gunners would have used to swab the inside of the cannon barrel, keeping it clear of gunpowder residue.

The palisade in front of the land face was being repaired when O'Sullivan made this exposure. A group of Union soldiers can be seen replacing damaged or destroyed pine timbers about halfway down the land face, left of center.

Soon after O'Sullivan shot this view of battery 2, his glass plate negative cracked. Faint double lines of the crack are noticeable in the center of the photograph. He then determined to re-shoot the image.

Land Face Batteries
(Interior)

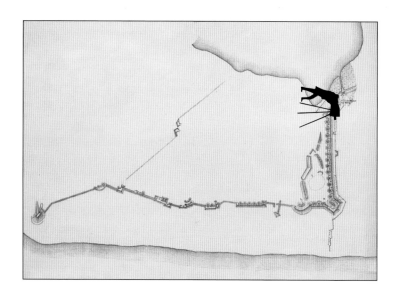

Photo by Daniel Ray Norris, January 1, 2011

Battery 2 (b)

Land Face Batteries
(Interior)

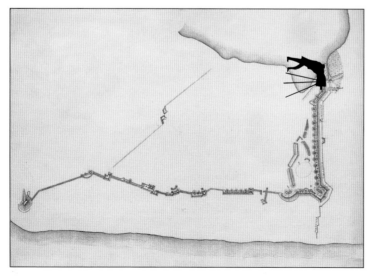

After cracking the first glass plate negative of the wrecked 8-inch shell gun in battery 2, O'Sullivan remounted Shepherd's Battery to take this stereoscopic view (LC-B11-1238). O'Sullivan repositioned his camera slightly further back on the first traverse, but otherwise the camera angle is virtually identical to the previous image on page 62. However, a little more marsh grass is visible in the left bottom corner and the iron canister and boxes on the terreplein are more obscured in this second photograph. The soldiers repairing the palisade have made good progress, while other men can be seen scattered along the top of the battle-scarred fort all the way to the Northeast Bastion in the background.

Battery 4

By all accounts, the hand-to-hand combat for possession of battery 4 and the fourth traverse was some of the most desperate of the second battle for Fort Fisher. Here a Confederate counterattack, comprised of soldiers led by Major General W.H.C. Whiting who had turned back the Union sailors and Marines' assault on the Northeast Bastion, slammed into the vanguard of U.S. Army troops advancing eastward along the land face rampart. Whiting was shot while struggling with a Union flag bearer, only to be rescued by his own men before the enemy could get to him. They took the general to the post hospital in Battery Meade, but he was too badly wounded to return to action. Whiting was taken captive when Fort Fisher fell later that night, and subsequently died as a prisoner of war at Fort Columbus, Governor's Island, New York, on March 10, 1865.[6]

Land Face Batteries
(Interior)

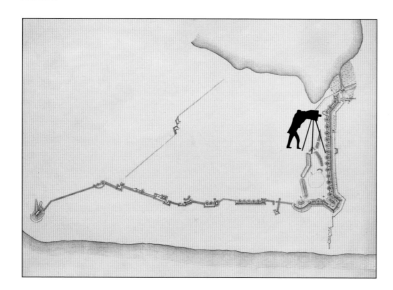

**Major General W.H.C. Whiting,
Confederate States Army**

A discarded cartridge box lies in the left foreground, and charred timbers, guncotton, and debris litter the area in the photograph (LC-B8171-7056). A disabled gun carriage can be seen in the water-filled pit, and another disabled one on the battery's terreplein, up against the traverse revetment. The 32-pounder cannon on the left side of the battery had its muzzle blown off by a Union navy projectile, although it remained mounted on the carriage. A pyramid of 32-pounder solid shot balls, with only the top ball missing, sits to the left of the cannon. A dismounted 24-pounder cannon lies on the terreplein to the right, and a full stack of 24-pounder balls is nearby, just above the broken steps. An armed guard leans jauntily against the battery's bombproof doorway.

Battery 6

**Land Face
Batteries**
(Interior)

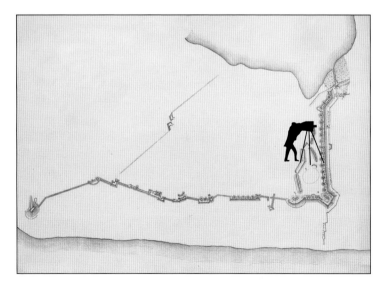

Although O'Sullivan did not specify the subject of this stereoscopic view (LC-B815-1242), it is probably battery 6 of Fort Fisher's land face defenses. According to ordnance records, the emplacement contained a 6.4-inch smoothbore gun and a 24-pounder Coehorn mortar. The dismounted piece of artillery shown here on the wood-paved terreplein is a U.S. Navy 6.4-inch, 32-pounder. The large metallic object underneath the chassis tongue, obscured by the left traverse, may well be the battery's mortar. A lone sentinel, rifle-musket in hand, poses for O'Sullivan.[7]

Battery 11

**Land Face
Batteries**
(Interior)

O'Sullivan took three photographs of battery 11 on Fort Fisher's land front. This stereoscopic image (LC-B811-1235) shows an unidentified Union soldier wearing an overcoat to ward off the cold of that early February 1865 day, shouldering a rifle-musket and standing still for the camera. He may be the same soldier pictured in battery 6 seen on page 68. Standing on wooden slats leading up to the battery's terreplein, he examines the destruction to a U.S. Navy 32-pounder gun carriage. Note that the trunnion of the dismounted cannon (left side of the terreplein) is broken off. The backside of the traverse in the right foreground shows river marsh grass planted on the slope to mitigate erosion.

Battery 11 (b)

O'Sullivan repositioned his camera a bit farther behind battery 11 than in the previous image, capturing in this photograph (LC-B817-7243) the imposing size and strength of the traverses that flanked the land face gun chamber. In the two largest naval bombardments of the Civil War, December 24-25, 1864, and January 13-15, 1865, Rear Admiral David D. Porter's warships fired approximately 40,000 shot and shell at Fort Fisher. Not a single projectile, including 15-inch spherical shells that weighed in excess of 300 pounds, penetrated the interior of a bombproof, each of which was covered by twelve to fifteen feet of beach sand and marsh sod.[8]

The Union soldier on the terreplein (different than the one pictured on page 70), gives some perspective as to the structure of the battery and its ordnance. Cradling a carbine under his left arm and wearing an overcoat, he peers at O'Sullivan's camera from beside the damaged 32-pounder gun carriage. In the back left corner of the gun emplacement (between the cannon barrel beside the left traverse and the soldier) is a stack of solid shot 32-pounder iron cannonballs.

Draped across the charred timber at the bottom of the steps in the foreground are pieces of discarded clothing and rags. What appears to be small cask lies in the immediate foreground left of center, while a soldier's forage cap rests on the slope of the traverse, to the right of the bottom step.

Land Face Batteries
(Interior)

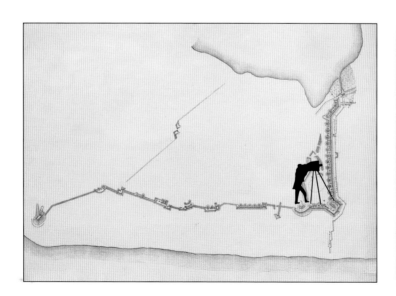

Battery 11 (c)

Land Face Batteries
(Interior)

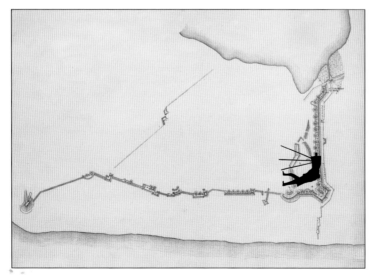

Standing atop the eleventh traverse looking westward, O'Sullivan pointed his camera toward the terreplein of battery 11 to make this stereoscopic image (LC-815-1239). The U.S. Navy 32-pounder cannon and carriage were heavily damaged, and the chassis knocked on its side by the Union bombardment of mid-January 1865. The mustached-soldier (the same one seen in the photograph on page 72) holds the butt end of a Model 1860 Spencer carbine as he looks up at O'Sullivan from the floor of the gun pit. The tall, lanky soldier gazing at the camera from atop the battery's revetment may be the same one pictured in Shepherd's Battery (b) on page 56 (second soldier left of the flagpole).

Battery 15

Land Face Batteries
(Interior)

There are two extant photographs of the interior of battery 15. The first, this stereoscopic view (LC-B815-1230), shows a rifled and banded U.S. Navy 6.4-inch, 32-pounder gun with its muzzle shot away. The breeching jaws on the rear of the cannon were also knocked off, and the right carriage wheel dented. Several stands of iron canister, partially covered by sand, lay beside the wooden revetment of the left traverse. An armed Union artillerist, as indicated by the cross cannon insignia on the crown of his forage cap, stands at attention behind the gun carriage. Companies B, G, and L, 1st Connecticut Artillery and Company A, 2nd Pennsylvania Heavy Artillery served as occupation forces at Fort Fisher in 1865.[9]

Battery 15 (b)

O'Sullivan mounted his camera atop the fourteenth traverse of Fort Fisher's land face to make this image (LC-B817-7061) of battery 15, looking eastward. It clearly shows the terrible effects of the U.S. Navy's shock and awe bombardment, January 13-15, 1865. A civilian wearing a rakish hat—possibly Timothy H. O'Sullivan himself—stands on the chassis of the damaged rifled and banded U.S. Navy 6.4-inch, 32-pounder cannon and looks northward up Confederate Point beach. Behind him on the chassis tongue is a vent pick, a tool used for punching holes in gunpowder cartridges through a hole in the breech of the cannon tube. Note that the floor of the terreplein is paved with planks.

On the far left is a group of six or seven soldiers. O'Sullivan's camera also managed to capture the broken muzzle of a 10-inch Columbiad in battery 16 and the Northeast Bastion in the background.

Land Face Batteries
(Interior)

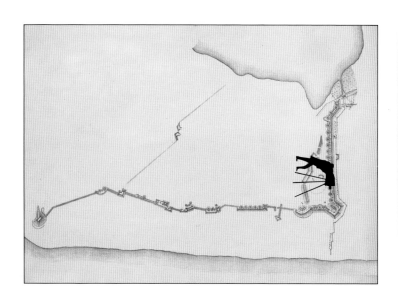

Artillery vent pick on the gun chassis tongue

Battery 16

Two 10-inch Columbiads were mounted on Fort Fisher's land face: one in the first gun chamber of Shepherd's Battery and the other (seen here), in battery 16. A Union navy projectile busted-off its muzzle in the January 1865 engagement. Three 10-inch cannonballs lie on the battery's sandy terreplein left of center in this half-stereoview (LC-B811-1233). Five Union soldiers pose for O'Sullivan's camera. The armed soldier standing at attention at the rear of the gun chassis in front of the sandbag wall is the same soldier in battery 15 as seen on page 76. The hat of the second man from the left standing on the traverse bears the insignia—a stamped brass castle—of an army engineer. Two companies of the 15th New York Engineers surveyed Fort Fisher under the direction of Brevet Brigadier General Cyrus B. Comstock.

10-inch cannonballs in battery 16

Land Face Batteries
(Interior)

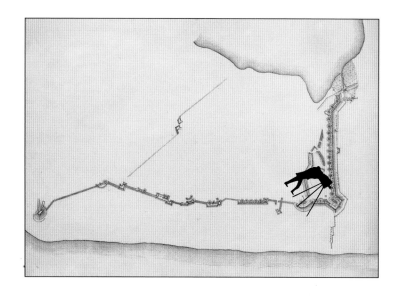

Civil War engineer's insignia

Northeast Bastion

Land Face Batteries
(Interior)

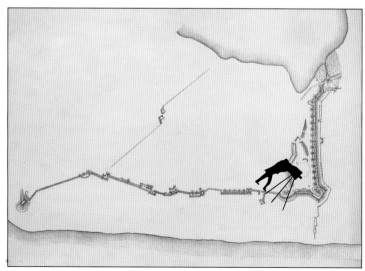

Two unidentified Union army officers survey the damage to the interior of the Northeast Bastion's bombproof and the first two sea face batteries. Standing atop an overturned gun chassis, the officer left of center gazes eastward. Behind his shoulders is a 10-inch seacoast mortar that lobbed shells on advancing Federal army troops on January 15, 1865. The breech of a mounted 10-inch Columbiad can be seen in the center gun emplacement of this stereoscopic view (LC-B811-1236). Projectiles of various makes and sizes and gun carriage parts litter the area. What appears to be a lost shoe lies in the sand in the far left foreground.

Cumberland Battery and Columbiad Battery

That the Federal fleet concentrated its intense fire on Fort Fisher's land face defenses during the January 1865 battle, with the objective of crippling the artillery covering the northern ground approaches to the fort, is apparent in this photograph (LC-B817-7335). Unlike the heavily damaged rampart and traverses on the land front, Cumberland and Columbiad batteries on the sea face show virtually no effects from the naval attack, with the exception of some unexploded cannonballs on the beachfront.

Cumberland Battery extended approximately fifty yards in front of the main line of Fort Fisher's sea face batteries, but was connected to it by a sand curtain. The redan rose only about eight feet above the beach. Armed with a massive 10-inch Columbiad, the battery was designed for ricochet firing across the ocean toward enemy vessels. The battery's

namesake is unknown, although Cumberland County was part of the Confederate military's District of the Cape Fear. Two soldiers sit on either side of the Columbiad.

South of Cumberland Battery was Columbiad Battery, a series of six artillery emplacements, separated by high sandy traverses, that paralleled the shoreline for approximately 135 yards. Each gun compartment (right to left) contained an 8-inch Columbiad, hence the battery's name, with the exception of the fifth chamber (south of the fifth traverse), which was armed with a double-banded 7-inch Brooke rifle. Two Brooke rifles were mounted in Columbiad Battery during the December 1864 battle, but both of them, commanded by a detachment of Confederate States Navy sailors, got overheated and burst and their carriages disabled.[10] Note the scarred beach in front of Columbiad Battery, where sand was excavated for the work's construction.

Sea Face Batteries
(Exterior)

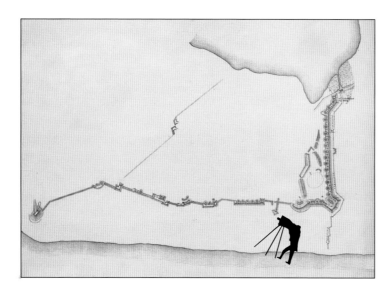

Battery Bolles and Battery Purdie

A heavy sand embankment connected Columbiad Battery with Battery Bolles and Battery Purdie (from right to left), as seen in this O'Sullivan image (LC-B817-7577). Battery Bolles, named for its designer and construction supervisor, Major Charles Pattison Bolles, was the first artillery position constructed on Confederate Point beginning on April 28, 1861. The Wilmington Light Infantry, commanded by Captain William Lord DeRosset, mounted two 24-pounder guns in Battery Bolles in early May 1861. Colonel William Lamb later replaced them with the two rifled and banded U.S. Navy 6.4 inch, 32-pounder guns, visible in this photograph.[11]

Courtesy of Adaire Graham

**Post-war photograph of
Charles Pattison Bolles**

Sea Face Batteries
(Exterior)

Battery Purdie flanked Battery Bolles about seventy yards to the south. It mounted only one piece of artillery—an 8-inch, 150-pounder Armstrong rifle-cannon.

Several U.S. Navy projectiles, including two 15-inch cannonballs (exposed by an outgoing tide), and numerous iron fragments litter the beach. A man bending over can be seen in the distance below the sand curtain that adjoined Battery Bolles and Battery Purdie.

Battery Lenoir, Telegraph Station, and Battery Hedrick

North Carolina Troops, 1861-'65

Colonel John J. Hedrick

Sea Face Batteries
(Exterior)

This O'Sullivan photograph (LC-B817-7573) shows—from right to left—Battery Lenoir, telegraph station, and Battery Hedrick along the line of Fort Fisher's sea face defenses. Battery Lenoir connected to Battery Rowland, of which there is no extant image, about fifty yards to the north. Two cannons were mounted in Battery Lenoir: a 7-inch Brooke rifle in the gun chamber on the battery's north side, and a 6.4-inch, 32-pounder rifle. Both of them are pictured in this view. As with most of Fort Fisher's sea face batteries, Lenoir was built comparatively low to the ground for ricochet firing.

A telegraph station was constructed about seventy yards below Battery Lenoir. The roof of a building—presumably the telegraph station—and several tents are visible behind the large sand mound in the center of the photograph.

About sixty yards south of the telegraph station stood Battery Hedrick, mounting two 10-inch Columbiads. Colonel Lamb named the battery in honor of John J. Hedrick, commandant of Fort Fisher from late January until June 28, 1862. Hedrick subsequently headed other Cape Fear military posts, including Fort Anderson and Fort Johnston on the west side of the Cape Fear River, and Fort Holmes on Bald Head Island at Old Inlet. He was promoted colonel of the 40th Regiment North Carolina Troops (3rd N.C. Artillery) in November 1863.[12]

At least fourteen cannonballs and numerous projectile fragments cover the beach. Two men appear to be salvaging scrap iron near the telegraph station's mound.

The Pulpit and Battery Meade

O'Sullivan documented the interior of Fort Fisher's sea face batteries adjacent to the Northeast Bastion, as well as the site of a terrible tragedy in this photograph (LC-B8171-7057). The soldier standing closest to the camera on the right marks the spot where Fort Fisher's main powder magazine exploded the morning after the battle, January 16, 1865. Reportedly, two drunken U.S. Marines, probably looking for souvenirs or more whiskey, wandered into the underground magazine and accidentally blew it up. The explosion killed and wounded about 130 Union and Confederate soldiers, sailors, and Marines who were sleeping on and around the giant sand bunker following the hard fighting of the previous day.

In the left center background are the first three gun emplacements of Fort Fisher's sea face defenses. From left to right, the armament comprised a 10-inch Columbiad, a rifled and banded U.S. Navy 6.4-inch, 32-pounder, and another 10-inch Columbiad. Columbiads were capable of firing projectiles up to 2.5 miles.

The taller battery in the right center background, atop which five Union soldiers stand, was built of the same massive character as the land face defenses. Because it resembled a preacher's perch, it was named the Pulpit. It mounted a 10-inch Columbiad, until a premature discharge dismounted the piece during the December 1864 battle. When O'Sullivan took this image, the Pulpit's Columbiad lay in the pool of water at the bottom of the battery's stairway. The battery served as Lamb's command headquarters during the January 1865 engagement.

To the far right is the post hospital, originally a casemate work named Battery Meade.

Sea Face Batteries
(Interior)

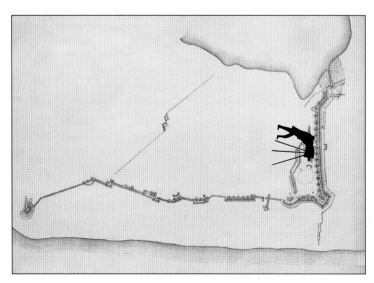

Frank Leslie's Illustrated Newspaper, February 11, 1865

Hospital (Battery Meade)

O'Sullivan made three views of Fort Fisher's hospital, which was incorporated into the sea face defenses. The crescent work was designed by Colonel Sewell Fremont in the summer of 1861 as an artillery position, with casemate embrasures for six cannon. Its construction was supervised by Captain John C. Winder, but the battery was named for Lieutenant Richard Kidder Meade Jr., one of the first military engineers at Fort Fisher. Meade had fought for the U.S. Army at Fort Sumter in Charleston harbor, April 12-14, 1861, but resigned his commission after that first battle of the war to join the Confederate Engineer Corps.

The palmetto timbers used in Battery Meade's construction eventually rotted, prompting Colonel Lamb to enclose the casemates, bombproof the structure using heavy pine beams, and turn it into the post hospital.[13]

Prewar view of Richard Kidder Meade Jr.

Sea Face Batteries
(Interior)

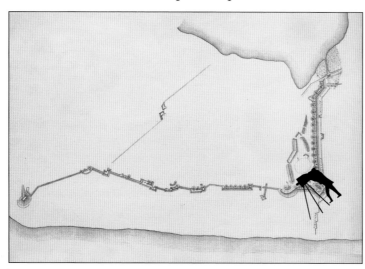

Looking eastward from the battery's parapet in this photograph (LC-B8171-7535), smoke wisps from the brick chimney in the foreground, while Union soldiers—their rifle-muskets neatly stacked—lounge outside the hospital on a bright, sunny early February morning. One soldier in the center of the image reads a newspaper, while two others sit along the ledge to the right, their backs up against the wooden revetment of an old gunpowder magazine.

The sand curtain that connected the line of sea face batteries with Cumberland Battery, the water battery near the ocean, can be seen on the far right.

Hospital (Battery Meade) (b)

Sea Face Batteries
(Interior)

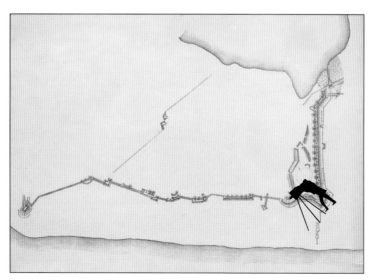

O'Sullivan moved across the covered way between the rampart and a former gunpowder magazine to make this stereoscopic view of Fort Fisher's hospital (LC-B815-1240). He apparently requested the large group of Union soldiers in the background to pose for the camera. They remained still long enough for O'Sullivan to take the time lapse photograph, otherwise any movement would have appeared as a blur in the image.

Ramrods for heavy artillery, and land mines—metallic barrels that would have been filled with gunpowder—lie unused nearby. Two officers confer on the parapet, while the soldier pictured on the far right peers down the line of sea face batteries to the south.

Hospital (Battery Meade) (c)

O'Sullivan shot this photograph (LC-B81221-4194) while standing on the hospital's south side. Wounded Confederate combatants, including General Whiting and Colonel Lamb, received medical attention here on January 15, 1865. As Union forces closed-in that night, Confederate soldiers evacuated their injured comrades to Battery Buchanan at the tip of Confederate Point where about 1,000 men, Whiting and Lamb among them, were ultimately captured.

In the foreground is a company of Union occupation troops, some of them curiously looking up at O'Sullivan while others chat as they stand in formation. Their ulsters (long overcoat with cape) reveal the cold weather that early February day. In the background, left of center, a lone soldier lies against the Pulpit battery.

Frank Leslie's Illustrated Newspaper, February 18, 1865

Wounded Union soldiers and Confederate prisoners inside Fort Fisher's bombproof hospital.

Sea Face Batteries
(Interior)

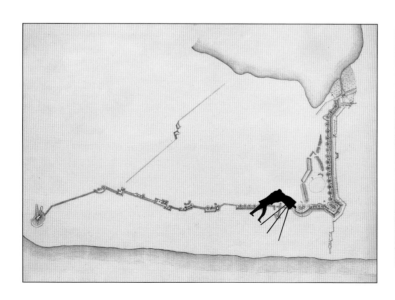

Columbiad Battery

This long range photograph (LC-B817-7101) looks eastward toward the rear of Columbiad Battery's six gun emplacements and traverses. The batteries were probably not built until 1864, as they do not appear on an 1863 Confederate engineers' map of Fort Fisher. Only the traverses of batteries 1 and 2 had been sodded, although blocks of river marsh grass were also being laid on the sixth traverse to the far right.

The large traverse on the far left served as the battery's gunpowder magazine. From left to right, the first four gun compartments each contained one 8-inch Columbiad.

The fifth gun chamber was armed with a 7-inch Brooke rifled cannon recovered from a sunken Confederate ironclad, CSS *Raleigh*, in the Cape Fear River. It overheated and burst during the fighting on Christmas Day, 1864. Another 8-inch Columbiad was mounted in the sixth battery on the far right. The Columbiads in gun chambers 1, 2, 4 and 6 are still mounted on their carriages and pointed in the direction of their last discharges in the battle of January 15, 1865.

At least eight unexploded Union navy cannonballs lie scattered about the sand plain in the foreground.

Sea Face Batteries
(Interior)

Dismounted 8-inch Columbiad in Columbiad Battery's third gun chamber, and battle wreckage.

Columbiad Battery (b)

A half-stereo view (LC-B811-1241) of Columbiad Battery's gun compartments 2–4 along the sea front. The guns in batteries 2 and 4 are turned on their center pintles and aimed toward the interior of Fort Fisher. As Union soldiers advanced onto the fort's parade ground behind the land face defenses late on the afternoon of January 15, 1865, Colonel William Lamb "went rapidly down the sea-face and turned. . .two Columbiads on this column." The 8-inch Columbiads were still in their final firing positions when O'Sullivan took this photograph about three weeks after the battle. The 8-inch Columbiad in battery 3 was dismounted and now lies on the terreplein.[14]

The cannon lying on the ground in the rear of battery 2 is an 8-inch Columbiad "in depot;" that is, the garrison intended to mount it in the battery. The interior slopes of the traverses were bolstered by bricks probably salvaged from a pre-war lighthouse that stood near the Northeast Bastion. The garrison dismantled the lighthouse in January 1863 to prevent Union gunboats from using it to establish an effective range of fire onshore.

Note the large debris field of iron projectile fragments and brickbats, as well as the damaged gun carriages and chassis behind the batteries.

Sea Face Batteries
(Interior)

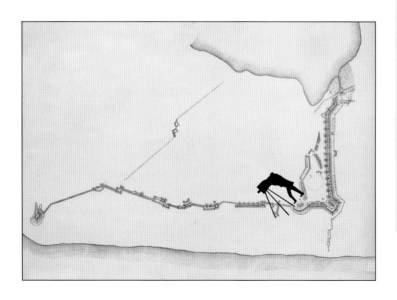

Colonel Lamb turned two 8-inch Columbiads, including this one in battery 2, on Union troops inside Fort Fisher on January 15, 1865.

Battery Purdie

O'Sullivan took two photographs of Battery Purdie on the sea face, as it boasted Fort Fisher's most famous piece of ordnance: an 8-inch, 150-pounder Armstrong rifle-cannon. Manufactured in Great Britain by W.G. Armstrong & Co., two sister Armstrong guns came in through the Union blockade of Wilmington on board the blockade-runner *Hope* in late August 1864. At General Whiting's request, the Confederate Ordnance Department in Richmond purchased the guns for Wilmington's defense. Whiting put one of the Armstrong guns in Fort Caswell at Old Inlet and the other in Fort Fisher.[15]

Colonel Lamb mounted Fort Fisher's Armstrong gun about halfway down the line of sea face batteries. Although generally referred to as the Armstrong Battery, it was officially named Battery Purdie in honor of Colonel

Courtesy of Alan Purdie

Thomas J. Purdie

Thomas J. Purdie, commander of the 18th Regiment North Carolina Troops, who was killed in action at the battle of Chancellorsville, Virginia, on May 3, 1863.[16]

The Armstrong gun came mounted on a mahogany and rosewood carriage that its crew claimed gave it the appearance of a piece of "parlor furniture" rather than a piece of artillery. Its carriage wheels were cast brass, and the manufacturers name and product number were painted on the rear of the chassis rail (far left).

A group of seventeen Union soldiers lounge on the battery's sun basked north traverse. The shadow of O'Sullivan and his camera darken the right foreground. Note the backside of Fort Fisher's land face batteries on the horizon.

Sea Face Batteries
(Interior)

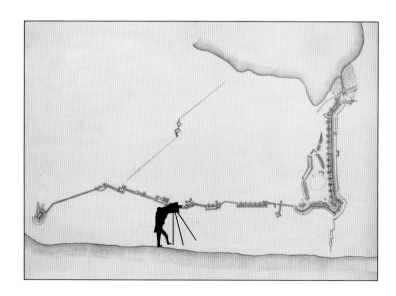

Battery Purdie (b)

Sea Face Batteries (Interior)

This stereoscopic view (LC-B811-1234) of the Armstrong gun also shows four inquisitive soldiers peering at O'Sullivan's camera. The musket-bearer at the rear of the gun chassis is a different soldier than the one in the image on page 102. That, along with the now overcast sky, suggests that the two images of the Armstrong gun were taken on different days. Cannon implements lean against the battery's wooden revetment to the left, and at least a dozen flattop and domed iron bolts lie on the terreplein behind the armed guard. The rope in the right foreground and the battery's interior slope appear to be covered with frost.

The victorious Union army seized Fort Fisher's Armstrong as a trophy of war and moved it to the grounds of the United States Military Academy at West Point, New York. It has been a key feature of the U.S. Army's impressive ordnance collection there since August 1865. The government temporarily loaned the Armstrong rifle-cannon to the Fort Fisher State Historic Site for a fifteen-month display in 2004-2006.

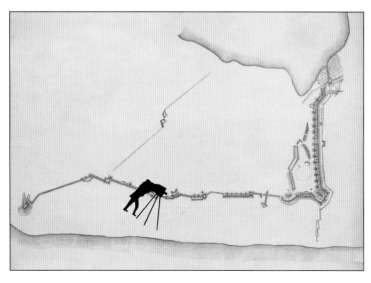

Battery Lamb

At the far south end of the sea face batteries stood Fort Fisher's most famous landmark—Battery Lamb, a massive conical work that served as both an artillery position and a signal station. O'Sullivan made three views of it, this one being LC-USC62-79428 in the Library of Congress' Prints and Photographs Collections.

Battery Lamb's two seacoast guns—a 10-inch Columbiad and a 7-inch Brooke rifle—provided covering fire for blockade-runners entering and exiting New Inlet, while the multicolor signal lights, which could be seen for miles at sea, offered them navigational assistance as they approached New Inlet.

Laborers built the imposing battery by transporting hundreds of cartloads of sand along a railway laid on an inclined ramp in the work's rear. After reaching the top,

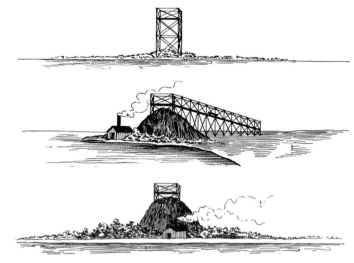

Official Records of the Union and Confederate Navies

they dumped the sand over the sides to fill-in around a tall wooden structure that served as both a bombproof and an ordnance magazine. Acting Rear Admiral S. Philips Lee, commander of the North Atlantic Blockading Squadron from 1862-1864, enclosed sketches of the Confederate battery under construction in his report to U.S. Secretary of the Navy Gideon Welles on April 17, 1863.

The signal lights' mount (left), Columbiad, and flagpole are visible on the summit of Battery Lamb. A chassis lies at the bottom of the sand ramp. The two large objects to the far right may be U.S. Navy gunboats in New Inlet almost one mile to the south.

Sea Face Batteries

(Interior)

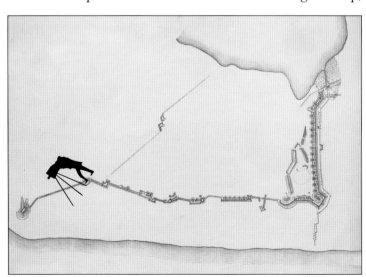

Battery Lamb (b)

Confederate military authorities named this imposing defensive work Battery Lamb in honor of Fort Fisher's respected and popular commander, Colonel William Lamb. However, both the officers and enlisted men of the garrison generally referred to it as Mound Battery because of its shape. It was, by far, the tallest feature in the fort. Lamb claimed in his postwar memoirs that the battery towered sixty feet above Confederate Point. In late January 1865, U.S. Army engineers calculated Battery Lamb's height as being only forty-three feet, and the photographic evidence seems to support their measurement.

The succession of O'Sullivan's images of Battery Lamb is unknown. In this view (LC-B817-7119) he positioned his camera closer to the work than in the previous image, but still pointing southward. Two Union soldiers stand

Colonel William Lamb

Sea Face Batteries
(Interior)

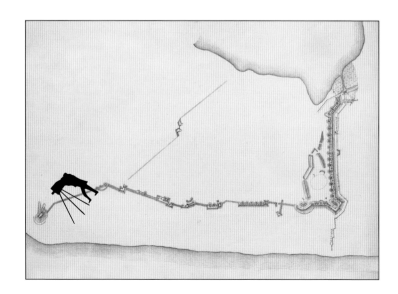

on the battery's summit, the 10-inch Columbiad behind them, while a sentry stands at the bombproof/ordnance magazine's doorway at the bottom of the stairway below.

Iron projectile fragments from the two U.S. Navy bombardments lie scattered across the sand plain, while a chassis and stack of 10-inch cannonballs rest on the ground at the bottom of the ramp in the far right background.

Battery Lamb (c)

The third photograph of Battery Lamb (LC-B817-7622) provides good clarity of the impressive sand work. His camera now located on the south side of the battery, O'Sullivan captured a chassis, perhaps the rail car used in the battery's construction in March and April 1863, at the bottom of the massive ramp, which would have been the first feature of the battery to be built.

A remarkable incident occurred at Battery Lamb during the battle on Christmas Eve, 1864. From his headquarters near the Northeast Bastion, Colonel Lamb noticed that the Union fleet was concentrating much of its fire on the fort's flags. The main flagstaff on the parade ground got so chewed-up by bursting shells that the garrison standard could not be raised. Lamb sent word to Captain Daniel Munn to hoist a flag on Mound Battery, way above the beach and in plain view of the enemy. As the flagpole was not equipped with halyards to secure the standard, Munn ordered Corporal Noah B. Bennett of Company K, 36th Regiment North Carolina Troops (2nd N.C. Artillery), to shinny the pole and attach it by hand. But Bennett, who weighed-in at 196 pounds, was too big to make the climb, so Private Christopher C. "Kit" Bland volunteered.

Bland quickly drew the wrath of Union warships as he undertook his ascent, but miraculously escaped being hit by incoming projectiles. In fact, he repeated his bold act amid the cheers of both his comrades and Union gunners after the lower end of the flag was cut away by a shell. The flag flew over Battery Lamb for the remainder of the battle, and was subsequently presented as a trophy of the Confederate victory to North Carolina Governor Zebulon B. Vance.

Sea Face Batteries
(Exterior)

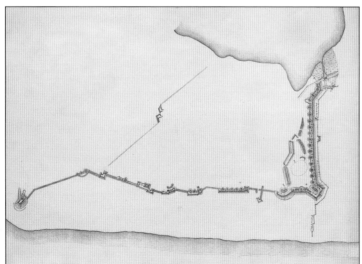

Battery Buchanan

O'Sullivan took two views of Battery Buchanan at the south tip of Confederate Point, about one mile southwest of Battery Lamb. Acting on orders from General Whiting, Colonel Lamb built Battery Buchanan in the autumn of 1864 to guard against any attempt by Union warships to push through New Inlet and into the Cape Fear River. The magnificent elliptical battery was based on a design furnished to Lamb by Redden Pittman, a young farmer-turned-engineer from Edgecombe County, North Carolina. Pittman hoped to call the work Battery Augusta after his sweetheart, but General Whiting instructed Lamb to name it Battery Buchanan in honor of Admiral Franklin Buchanan of the Confederate States Navy, who was captured at the battle of Mobile Bay, Alabama, on August 5, 1864.[19]

Library of Congress

**Admiral Franklin Buchanan,
Confederate States Navy**

**South tip of
Confederate
Point**

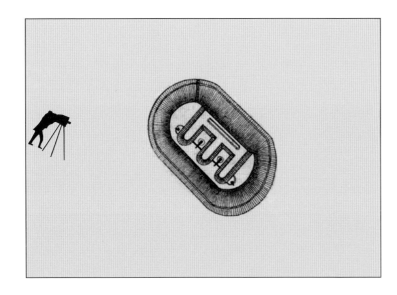

The formidable battery mounted four seacoast cannons—two 11-inch Brooke smoothbores and two 10-inch Columbiads—separated by three massive connected traverses, with direct fire across New Inlet. The Brooke guns are pictured on the left side of the battery, the Columbiads to the right. Battery Buchanan was also a citadel to which Fort Fisher's garrison might retreat or reinforcements sent, as a wharf nearby could accommodate even large steamships. The battery was manned by a detachment of Confederate sailors and Marines.

Fourteen Union soldiers stand atop the battery's parapet, all looking toward O'Sullivan's camera positioned in a mud flat south of the work. Note the mule-drawn dray on the far left.

Battery Buchanan (b)

South tip of Confederate Point

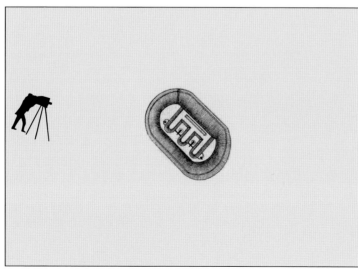

For his second image of Battery Buchanan, O'Sullivan made a stereoscopic view (LC-B815-1231) from a position farther back on the mud flat near New Inlet. Five soldiers are atop the battery's parapet, while four other soldiers can be made out beside the Brooke rifle, second gun from the left. Yet another soldier stands on the beach looking toward the camera. The mule-drawn dray is more visible here (left of center) than in the previous image on page 112. On the far left is a U.S. Army encampment, as indicated by the numerous pup tents and large A-frame tents. The masts and smokestacks of two ships in New Inlet are visible on the far right side of the photograph.

Quartermaster's Office, Fort Fisher, N.C.

The exact location of the clapboard structure in this photograph is unknown, as it no longer stands. O'Sullivan identified it as the "Quartermaster's Office, Fort Fisher, N.C." It apparently served as a dual office building, as the sign on the right side of the porch reads "Quartermaster's Office," and the other "Depot Commissary."

Most of the buildings inside Fort Fisher were destroyed by the naval bombardments, so the post quartermaster's office/commissary depot doubtfully survived. A likely location for this structure was near Battery Buchanan at the tip of Confederate Point (Union engineers designated it Ft. Buchanan on their survey map). That area was not heavily targeted by Union warships, and the faint outline of what may be an earthwork appears on the far left side of the photograph.

Another possible spot for the building was about 1.5 miles north of Fort Fisher in the rear of the U.S. Army's fortified encampment on the grounds of old Confederate Camp Wyatt. Engineers pinpointed the "Commissary," circled in blue, on its "Sketch of Vicinity of Fort Fisher" map.

None of the men or the African American sailor boy (standing on the far right of the porch) in the image have been identified. The man in civilian dress smoking a pipe in the center of the photograph seems to be the focus of O'Sullivan's camera. He looks somewhat like Brevet Major General Alfred H. Terry (see page 25), but his comparatively small stature (Terry stood 6' 2" tall) negates that possibility. Army tents can be seen on both sides of the building.

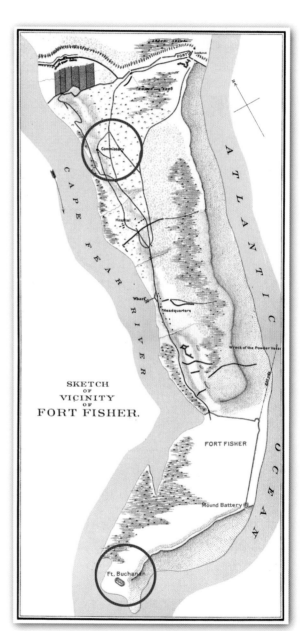

The Official Military Atlas of the Civil War

Miscellaneous Photographs

Courtesy of Barbara Baker

Written in pencil on the reverse of this stereoscopic card is "Federal Pt. NC." If the provenance is accurate, T.H. O'Sullivan may well have taken the photograph that shows at least eight ships in the offing.

This image is identified in the Library of Congress' Prints and Photographs Collections as "Fort Fisher, NC, interior view" (LC-B815-1138), and consequently has been reprinted in several publications as such. It is not Fort Fisher. In fact, it is a photograph of Confederate Fort Darling on Drewry's Bluff along the James River below Richmond, Virginia. For comparative views of Fort Darling see LC-B811-3352 and LC-DIG-cwpb-00045, accessible through the Library of Congress' homepage.

Library of Congress

Fort Fisher State Historic Site

This photograph of a rippled mud flat and what appears to be a large cannon on the horizon is in the holdings of the Fort Fisher State Historic Site. Its provenance is unknown, but the view is reminiscent of T.H. O'Sullivan's artistic photos of the American West taken in the early 1870s.

Endnotes

The Fort

1. United States Navy Department, *Official Records of the Union and Confederate Navies* 30 volumes [Washington, D.C., Government Printing Office, 1884-1922], series I, volume 4, 156-157, 340 (hereafter cited as *ORN* with all references to series I unless otherwise noted).

2. Chris E. Fonvielle Jr., *The Wilmington Campaign: Last Rays of Departing Hope* (Campbell, California: Savas Publishing, 1997), 8-13 (hereafter cited as Fonvielle, *The Wilmington Campaign*).

3. Stephen R. Wise, *Lifeline of the Confederacy: Blockade Running During the Civil War* (Columbia: University of South Carolina Press, 1988), 287.

4. Fonvielle, *The Wilmington Campaign*, 20-22.

5. Bolles to Curtis, March 26, 1901, Charles P. Bolles Papers, Office of Archives and History, Raleigh, North Carolina.

6. Charles Force Deems, *Autobiography of Charles Force Deems* (New York: Fleming H. Revell Company, 1897), 175 (hereafter cited as Deems, *Autobiography*); *Wilmington Daily Journal*, September 19, 1873.

7. Order No. 1, August 31, 1861, General Correspondence, 1861-1893, Dorothy F. Grant Papers, N.C. State Archives, Raleigh; Fremont to Clark, August 31, 1861, Governor Henry T. Clark Papers, Office of Archives and History, Raleigh, North Carolina; *Wilmington Daily Journal*, August 31, 1861.

8. *Wilmington Daily Journal*, February 1, 1862, September 19, 1873; William Lamb, *Colonel Lamb's Story of Fort Fisher* (Carolina Beach, N.C.: The Blockade Runner Museum, 1966), 1 (hereafter cited as *Colonel Lamb's Story of Fort Fisher*).

9. *Wilmington Daily Journal*, September 14, 1861; Bolles to DeRosset, October 11, 1906, Charles P. Bolles Papers, N.C. State Archives, Raleigh; Louis Manarin, Weymouth T. Jordan, Jr., Matthew M. Brown, and Michael W. Coffey, eds., *North Carolina Troops 1861-1865: A Roster* 19 volumes (Raleigh, North Carolina: Office of Archives and History, Raleigh, North Carolina, 1966-2013), Jordan, vol. 4, 267 [hereafter cited as *North Carolina Troops*].

10. Walter Clark, ed., *Histories of the Several Regiments and Battalions From North Carolina in the Great War, 1861-'65*, 5 volumes (Wendell, N.C.: Broadfoot's Bookmark reprint, 1982), vol. V, 23-28; *Wilmington Daily Herald,* February 16, 1861; Manarin, *North Carolina Troops*, vol. I, 218-219. The namesake of Shepherd's Battery is unknown. Ray Flowers, site interpreter at the Fort Fisher State Historic Site, speculates that "because of the battery's isolated location when it was built, it resembled a shepherd's retreat" (interview with Ray Flowers, Wilmington, North Carolina, July 8, 2010). Colonel Lamb referred to it in his memoir as "Shepperd's Battery" (*Colonel Lamb's Story of Fort Fisher*, 1). It seems unlikely that the battery was named for Dr. Joseph C. Shephard, post surgeon at Fort Fisher beginning in the autumn of 1864. The battery was already in place when Lamb arrived at Fort Fisher on July 4, 1862. See also: James Sprunt, *Chronicles of the Cape Fear River 1660-1916* (Wilmington, North Carolina: Broadfoot Publishing Company reprint, 1992), 361.

11. William Lamb, "The Defense of Fort Fisher," in Robert U. Johnson and Clarence C. Buel, eds., *Battles and Leaders of the Civil War* 4 volumes (New York: The Century Company, 1884, 1888), vol. 4, 643; *Colonel Lamb's Story of Fort Fisher*, 1-5; Report of Cyrus B. Comstock, January 27, 1865, *The War of the Rebellion, A Compilation of the Official Records of the Union and Confederate Armies* 128 volumes (Washington, D.C.: Government Printing Office, 1880-1901), series I, volume 46, 406-408 (hereafter cited as *ORA* with all references to series I unless otherwise noted). See also: Fonvielle, *The Wilmington Campaign*, 43-45.

The Battles

1. Craig L. Symonds, ed., *Union Combined Operations in the Civil War* (New York: Fordham University Press, 2010), 101-102 (hereafter cited as Symonds, *Union Combined Operations in the Civil War*); Gideon Welles, *Diary of Gideon Welles* 3 vols. (Boston and New York, 1911), vol. 2, 127.

2. Grant to Stanton, July 22, 1865, *ORN* 11, 358-359; Report of David D. Porter, December 26, 1864, *ORN* 11, 254; Paul H. Silverstone, *Warships of the Civil War Navies* (Annapolis, Maryland: Naval Institute Press, 1989), 15 (hereafter cited as Silverstone, *Warships of the Civil War Navies*).

3. Fonvielle, *The Wilmington Campaign*, 80-82.

4. *Richmond Enquirer*, October 26, 1864; William Lamb, "The Battles of Fort Fisher," *Southern Historical Society Papers* 52 vols. (1876-1959), vol. 21, 266 (hereafter cited as Lamb, "The Battles of Fort Fisher, *SHSP*).

5. Benjamin F. Butler, *Butler's Book* (Boston: A.M. Thayer, 1892), 775-776; A.C. Rhind, "The Last of the Powder Boat," *United States Service Magazine* (April 1879), 230-231; Thomas O. Selfridge, Jr., *Memoirs of Thomas O. Selfridge, Jr.* (New York: Knickerbocker Press, 1924), 122; Fonvielle, *The Wilmington Campaign*, 121-126.

6. Lamb, "The Battles of Fort Fisher," *SHSP*, vol. 21, 269; *Colonel Lamb's Story of Fort Fisher*, 14.

7. *Colonel Lamb's Story of Fort Fisher*, 35; *Wilmington Messenger*, June 15, 1893; Porter to Welles, January 20, 1865, *ORN* 11, 620.

8. Lamb to Hill, December 27, 1864, *ORA* 42, pt. 1, 1004; *New York Herald*, December 31, 1864.

9. Report of William Lamb, December 27, 1864, *ORA* 42, pt. 1, 1006; Lamb, "The Battles of Fort Fisher," *SHSP* 21, 271; *Colonel Lamb's Story of Fort Fisher*, 16.

10. Fonvielle, *The Wilmington Campaign*, 172.

11. Fonvielle, *The Wilmington Campaign*, 180-181.

12. Symonds, *Union Combined Operations in the Civil War*, 105-106; John Y. Simon, ed., *The Papers of Ulysses S. Grant* (Carbondale and Edwardsville: Southern Illinois University Press), vol. 13, 131, 169 (hereafter cited as Simon, *The Papers of Ulysses S. Grant*).

13. Symonds, *Union Combined Operations in the Civil War*, 106-108.

14. Unpublished memoir of David D. Porter, Library of Congress, Washington, D.C.

The Photographer

1. Detailed report of Rear-Admiral Porter, *ORN* 11, 480; *New York Tribune*, January 26, 1865.

2. Simon, *The Papers of Ulysses S. Grant*, vol. 13, 278, 520.

3. James D. Horan, *Timothy O'Sullivan: America's Forgotten Photographer* (New York: Bonanza Books, 1966).

4. *New York Herald*, February 8, 1865.

The Photographs

1. Fonvielle, *The Wilmington Campaign*, 108; Silverstone, *Warships of the Civil War Navies*, 15.

2. In his postwar memoir, Colonel William Lamb referred to it as Shepperd's Battery, but period maps and official correspondence labeled it Shepherd's Battery. See: *Colonel Lamb's Story of Fort Fisher*, 1; Fort and adjoining fortifications, with note, 1863, Gilmer Civil War Maps, Southern Historical Collection, University of North Carolina, Chapel Hill; McCormic to Parker, December 29, 1864, *ORA* 46, pt. 1, 1011.

3. Extract from the official diary of Colonel Lamb, C.S. Army, commanding the defenses of Confederate (Federal Point) with headquarters at Fort Fisher, January 12, 1865, *ORN* 11, 596; H.J. Keith, *The Guns of Fort Fisher: A Pictorial Study of Ordnance From the Imagery of Timothy O'Sullivan* (Eagle, Idaho: Novus Development Corporation, 2009), 48-49 (hereafter cited as Keith, *The Guns of Fort Fisher*).

4. Fonvielle, *The Wilmington Campaign*, 237, 258.

5. Fonvielle, *The Wilmington Campaign*, 269-272.

6. Fonvielle, *The Wilmington Campaign*, 276, 281.

7. Keith, *The Guns of Fort Fisher*, 30-31.

8. Fonvielle, *The Wilmington Campaign*, 306.

9. *History of the First Connecticut Artillery and of the Siege Trains of the Armies Against Richmond, 1862-1865* (Hartford, Connecticut: Case, Lockwood & Brainard Company, 1893), 131.

10. Report of John C. Little, December 30, 1864, *ORA* 42, pt. 1, 1007.

11. Bolles to Curtis, March 26, 1901, Charles P. Bolles Papers, Office of Archives and History, Raleigh, North Carolina; Deems, *Autobiography*, 175; *Wilmington Daily Journal*, September 19, 1873.

12. *Colonel Lamb's Story of Fort Fisher*, 2.

13. *Wilmington Daily Journal*, February 1, 1862, September 19, 1873; *Colonel Lamb's Story of Fort Fisher*, 1.

14. *Colonel Lamb's Story of Fort Fisher*, 33.

15. Whiting to Gorgas, September 7, 1864, Letters Sent, District of the Cape Fear, Gen. W.H.C. Whiting's Command, Chp. 11, Vol. 338, August 1864-January 1865, Record Group 109, National Archives, Washington, D.C.

16. Jordan, *North Carolina Troops*, vol. VI, 305-306.

17. Report of Colonel William Lamb, December 27, 1864, *ORA* 46, pt. 1, 1006; United Confederate Veterans, Brunswick County Camp ledger, 41, Lewis Hardee Jr. Collection, Randall Library, UNC Wilmington; *Colonel Lamb's Story of Fort Fisher*, 16; Fonvielle, *The Wilmington Campaign*, 135-136.

18. Lee to Welles, *ORN* 8, 812-813.

19. *Colonel Lamb's Story of Fort Fisher*, 4-5; Fonvielle, *The Wilmington Campaign*, 45.

Glossary

Banded gun: an artillery piece reinforced with a layer of iron around its breech (rear of the tube).

Barbette: cannon mounted "en barbette," are seated on a high carriage, for firing over a parapet.

Bastion: work consisting of two faces and two flanks forming a salient angle.

Battery: a battery consists of two or more pieces of artillery. The term also refers to an emplacement where artillery is mounted for either defensive or offensive purposes.

Blockade-runner: Confederate ships and those of neutral nations, mainly British, employed in the profitable though risky violation of trading goods through the Union naval blockade of Southern seaports. The term also applied to captains, crews, shippers, and agents engaged in the trade.

Bolt: solid iron cylindrical projectile designed to penetrate or knock down a target.

Bombproof: reinforced bunker built underneath a fortification to provide protection for troops during a bombardment.

Breeching jaws: A semicircular attachment to the base or breech of a navy cannon into which a rope is inserted to arrest recoil during firing.

Canister: field artillery canister comprised a tin cylinder attached to a sabot and filled with small lead or iron shot.

Carriage: a gun carriage is designed to support a cannon, especially when fired. A seacoast gun carriage sat on a chassis, comprised of two rails and a tongue.

Carriage cheeks: supporting braces of a gun carriage on which trunnions are placed.

Casemate: vaulted chamber with embrasures for cannons.

Covered Way: a walkway, hidden from view by a rampart.

Curtain: part of a rampart joining batteries, bastions, or flanks.

Demilune: crescent-shaped outwork attached to the main fortification so as to cover the rampart with enfilade fire. Also termed a *ravelin*.

Embrasure: opening cut in a fortification's rampart or wall through which artillery could fire.

Enfilade: to sweep the length of a work or line of troops by artillery or small arms fire.

Fortification: consists in part of a mound of dirt called a *rampart* that encloses the body of the place, a *parapet* that surmounts the rampart, and *traverses*, mounds higher than the parapet that cross the breadth of the covered way.

Grapeshot: iron balls stacked between two iron plates and rings, and attached with a long pin and nut for use in seacoast guns.

Magazine: a bombproof structure for storing gunpowder and ammunition.

Ordnance: artillery, cannon.

Ordnance stores: cannonballs, shot, shell, and artillery equipment.

Palisade: timbered fence, usually sharpened, erected for defensive purposes.

Parapet: top or crest of a rampart (see *Fortification*).

Postern: passageway constructed underneath a rampart allowing for communication and transportation between the outside and inside of a fortification.

Rampart: wall of earth that protects a fortified place (see *Fortification*).

Ravelin: (see *Demilune*).

Redan: small work with two faces terminating in a salient angle to cover an encampment, advanced posts, front of a fort, approaches, bridges, etc.

Revetment: retaining wall designed to support the interior slope of the parapet, rampart, or traverse.

Rifle-gun: cannon whose muzzle has spiral grooves to provide greater distance and accuracy when fired.

Salient: a salient angle projecting away from the fortification.

Scarp (Escarp): interior side of the ditch.

Shell: hollow projectile, spherical or cylindrical, filled with gunpowder and armed with a fuse designed to detonate the projectile over a target or upon impact.

Smoothbore: cannon whose muzzle is smooth, without rifling.

Solid shot: solid iron cannonball designed to pierce or knock down a target.

Terreplein: flat surface of the rampart where artillery is mounted.

Traverse: mound of earth higher than the parapet which shields artillerists and gun chambers from enfilade fire along the line of a work (see *Fortification*).

Trunnion: two short cylinders projecting from the cannon tube by which it rests upon a carriage.

The Atlantic Ocean's unrelenting encroachment, storms, and time have finally done what the two largest Union naval bombardments of the Civil War did not: reduce Fort Fisher's massive earthen ramparts. The U.S. Army also played a big role when, in 1940, it established an advanced anti-aircraft training base at the old Confederate fort. The army cut an airstrip through the middle of Fort Fisher's land face to allow small planes to land. Today only about 20 percent of what was once the largest and strongest seacoast fortification in the Confederacy remains.

Courtesy of U.S. Army Corps of Engineers and Fort Fisher State Historic Site

Current Atlantic Ocean shoreline at the Fort Fisher State Historic Site with overlay of Confederate Fort Fisher.

Photo by Daniel Ray Norris, January 1, 2011

The Fort Fisher State Historic Site comprises almost 260 acres. Its rich Civil War and World War II history and natural habitat attracts about 500,000 people annually, making it by far the most visited historic site in North Carolina. About half of the fort's land face defenses are extant, including Shepherd's Battery (seen here), where Union and Confederate soldiers fought bravely on January 15, 1865. Colonel William Lamb wrote in 1893 that he confidently believed the time would come when the people of the Old North State would regard the battles of Fort Fisher as the grandest events of her historic past.